MEMOIRS OF AN
ITALIAN
TERRORIST

Also by Antony Shugaar

*America Discovered: The Guidebook Columbus
Should Have Had* (with Gianni Guadalupi)

Latitude Zero: Tales of the Equator
(with Gianni Guadalupi)

New York, The City that Never Sleeps

San Francisco, The City by the Bay

Translations

*The Judge and the Historian: Marginal Notes on a Late-
Twentieth-Century Miscarriage of Justice*
by Carlo Ginzburg

Niccolo's Smile: A Biography of Machiavelli
by Maurzio Viroli

Republicanism by Maurzio Viroli

Bios Theoretikos: A Biography of Aristotle by Carlo Natali

Western Medical Thought from Antiquity to the Middle Ages
edited by Mirko Grmek

Pasta: The Story of a Universal Food by Silvano Serventi
and Françoise Sabban

MEMOIRS OF AN
ITALIAN
TERRORIST

GIORGIO

TRANSLATED WITH AN INTRODUCTION
BY ANTONY SHUGAAR

Foreword
by Neal Ascherson

CARROLL & GRAF PUBLISHERS
NEW YORK

MEMOIRS OF AN ITALIAN TERRORIST

Carroll & Graf Publishers
An Imprint of Avalon Publishing Group Inc.
161 William St., 16th Floor
New York, NY 10038

Copyright © 1981 by SEMIR

First Carroll & Graf trade paperback edition 2003

Originally published in Italy as *Memorie dalla clandestinità un terrorista non pentito si racconta* in 1981

Translation © copyright 2003 by Antony Shugaar

Foreword copyright © 2003 by Neal Ascherson

Introduction copyright © 2003 by Antony Shugaar

Library of Congress Cataloging-in-Publication Data is available.

ISBN: 0-7867-1134-5

Book design by Paul Paddock
Printed in the United States of America
Distributed by Publishers Group West

CONTENTS

The author of this memoir is anonymous, known to his Italian publishers only as Giorgio. It is impossible to say to whom he would have dedicated this book. As the translator of the memoir into English and as the author of the introduction, I would like to dedicate my share of this book to my parents Carl and Gerda, my wife Lisa, and my daughter Arlie Tallulah.

I would like to acknowledge the kind assistance of Leo Sisti and Giulio Savelli.

FOREWORD

I t was on a dark December evening in Rome, almost precisely thirty-three years ago, that I heard the bang. An Italian friend was talking excitedly to me about the "strategy of tension," the supposed maneuver of President Saragat to raise fear of left-wing violence to the point of hysteria. My friend had a curious gesture—maybe Neapolitan—to denote intrigue: he revolved his finger rapidly by his ear and let out a whirring noise, like the sound of a clockwork spring unwinding. "Eeeeeeh!" he went. At that point, the windows jumped and the curtains bellied.

We ran out to see. Somebody had bombed the "wedding cake" Vittorio Emmanuele monument. The blast had knocked a few slivers of white marble off its plinth. I still keep a splinter, now worn smooth and golden, in my pocket.

Italy was entering the most sinister passage in its postwar history. The Rome bombs amounted to little. It was the simultaneous slaughter near the Piazza Fontana in Milan, where a bomb in a crowded farmers' bank killed sixteen people, that pitched the nation into a whirling darkness of rumor and conspiracy—including state conspiracy against the nation itself.

Who was doing what to whom? Nobody knew then, and nobody knows for sure now. The Piazza Fontana bomb was proclaimed to be a left-wing outrage. But it soon began to smell more like a neo-Fascist provocation, contrived to justify the arrest of anarchists and revolutionaries and to prepare public opinion for a military coup d'etat. This putsch was being organized with the help of the military dictatorship in Greece and, conceivably, with the encouragement of American intelligence. Was NATO involved? Were the Italian Communists, marching in public for the defense of democracy, secretly in league with the Christian Democrats and "dark forces" of the ultra-right in order to get rid of their own enemies on the ultra-left? Was anything what it seemed?

This is Giorgio's world. His extraordinary memoir of life underground in the years of the Red Brigades reflects all that fog of ambiguity. The comrade provides you with a gun, but is he a revolutionary or a provocateur? You fire the gun at a policeman, but how can you be sure that he is not a secret proletarian "entrist" into the forces of repression? Giorgio joins the underground under the assumption that he is joining the Red Brigades. Yet he discovers that he has become one of the "autonomi," an existentialist gunman sure only of himself and his tiny cell. In the same way, his memoir is almost certainly genuine, but just possibly might not be. Personally, I am pretty certain that Giorgio was who he says he was, not least because of the unselfconscious details about his life. His account conveys wonderfully the sinister frivolity of Italian urban terrorism. Weighty consideration is given to which style of trattoria a terrorist with street-cred should patronize. An engineer in the service of late-capitalism is marked down for assassination by Giorgio and his movements are obsessively trailed, but when it turns out that he has a secret mistress, his life is spared. A long, ironic passage discusses the erotic component of pinball, played by urban guerrillas in Milanese cafés in the intervals of clandestine "Workers' Power" meetings.

The fact is that Giorgio is a sophisticated, accomplished, and "literary" writer. He uses the rhythms and economies of the best Italian realist fiction. He tells you a great deal about his states of mind and his relationships, but he is reticent about the "actions" in which he has been involved and almost totally omits the "armed struggle" ideology that he and his comrades must have argued over every night. I find that reticence of his, over matters which would have made exciting reading, good evidence for the authenticity of Giorgio's book.

He certainly makes no effort to appear heroic, or even likeable. Giorgio presents himself as a cold, clever, self-obsessed personality; he worries more about his own inability to form relationships than about the widows and children of those he murders. Not all the boys and girls who took to the gun in those years were like him. Many were impulsive and passionate, and dreamed that they were liberators. But without the reliable Giorgios, those who hid in the underground in order to hide from themselves, Europe's most spectacular terrorist movement in the late twentieth century could never have darkened Italy with fear and confusion.

—Neal Ascherson
London, December 2002

INTRODUCTION

I n the large cities of northern Italy twenty-five years ago, it could be dangerous simply to go to work in the morning. For midlevel managerial types in the northwestern manufacturing city of Turin, where Fiat is located, in particular, the morning rush hour was a time of white-knuckle tension. This was when the terrorists struck, when they did their kneecapping and killing, and the targets of choice were midlevel managers. They fell victim to precisely the sort of political analysis that Giorgio describes in this memoir; and the terrorists effectively accomplished their purposes. After all, when the head of the company or the prime minister is killed by terrorists, very few are afraid that the same fate will be inflicted upon them; but when a colleague or someone in a position similar to their own is killed or kneecapped, the message, as it were, comes home.

As so often happens, chronic tension breeds black humor. The joke went, in the late 1970s, that a typical morning routine for a midlevel Fiat executive was as follows: get out of bed, turn on radio, shower, shave, drink cappuccino and eat biscuits, knot tie and button suit jacket, and when the radio announces that a midlevel Fiat executive has just been kneecapped or murdered somewhere else in the city, don overcoat and leave for work.

The kneecapping and killing of corporate executives— along with judges and policemen, journalists and university professors—had become by the mid-seventies part of a grim routine. The point of the joke is that the news flashes about terrorist attacks functioned as a sort of tacit weather report or traffic bulletin. The ghoulish humor lost its point the morning that there were two attacks in Turin; the joke vanished from circulation.

These memoirs, written and submitted anonymously in 1980 to a small alternative publisher in northern Italy, are truly a message in a bottle. The author, who identifies himself only as Giorgio, presumably his nom de guerre, or *nome di battaglia*, describes the path that led him to terrorism, offers a number of veiled accounts of actual terrorist attacks in which he took part, and provides gripping and devastating vignettes of the isolation and squalor that characterizes the terrorist's life.

In many ways, Giorgio's memoirs from underground speak for themselves, but this introduction is an attempt to provide context and annotation to a remarkable text. The terrorism in which Giorgio took part was distinctly Italian; it is not the bizarre, free-form American terrorism of the Weather Underground, the Symbionese Liberation Army, MOVE, or any of a variety of homegrown groups. Nor is it the Islamic religious fundamentalist terrorism that now stalks the world like a specter.

The Italian terrorism of the seventies and eighties was definitely Marxist-Leninist in inspiration, but it also took its methods, its names (the name Red Brigades harks back to the nomenclature of the Italian Resistance, as well as to the anti-Fascist Lincoln Brigades of the Spanish Civil War), and its moral justification from the less well known but very substantial Italian Resistance movement during World War II.

Fear spread throughout Italian society as the terrorists ratcheted their attacks upward. A psychological study done around this time by the Rand Corporation developed a sort of professional profile from a sampling of terrorists; interestingly, the profile closely matched that for professional athletes. The purpose of terrorism, and the mind-set of those who foment it, is a brutal treadmill in more ways than one: the goal is always to expand, always to better your last record. This is what makes it so terrifying, to use the obvious term, to be on the receiving end of a terrorist's efforts.

In the period of time described in these memoirs, the terrorists were indeed ratcheting their attacks upward, "raising their fire," as the expression went or, to use another expression common at the time, "taking their attack to the heart of the state."

The result of this campaign of escalation was a society-wide chill, and Italians still refer to this period—the heart of it extended from 1975 to 1981, the year in which these memoirs were published—as the Years of Lead. This is a clear reference to the bullets that killed close to five hundred people—there were nearly eight thousand terrorist attacks—in a slow-burning civil war that bloodied the cobblestones of Italy; it is also a classical reference to Hesiod's *Works and Days*, in which a Golden Age is followed by a Silver Age and ultimately an Age of Lead.

In 1977, the German newsweekly *Der Spiegel* ran a famous cover photograph of a black revolver on a plate of spaghetti. Italy became the sick man of Europe, crippled by labor unrest, social division, rocketing inflation, and terrorism. Fiat was one of the choice targets (for a number of reasons, but primarily because Fiat was the single largest company in Italy, accounting at one point for 4 percent of the country's GNP), and so hard hit was Fiat by the crippled economy, the rising cost of labor, and the general shortage of oil that 10 percent of the company was sold to a foreign investor: none other than Muammar Qadafi's Libyan state oil company.

Classic terrorist attacks aside, there was a steady drumbeat of partisan violence throughout society. Even before demonstrators marched through city streets shaking their right hands over their heads, thumb cocked and index finger extended, chanting ``P-38! P-38!'' the *chiave inglese*, or monkey wrench, was a fearsome tool, both in demonstrations and in early morning *pestaggi*, savage beatings that often resulted in death. The victims were, in the early days of the mid-1970s, more often members of the right-wing radical groups that opposed the left-wing extraparliamentarian demonstrators than professors or policemen. The monkey wrenches in question were not the ones with which the average American is familiar. They were huge affairs, often eighteen inches long, solid stainless steel, weighing ten or fifteen pounds,

and probably used to tighten bolts on hydroelectric tur-
bines. The Italian radical movement prided itself on its
proletarian roots and really did consist of as many blue-
collar factory workers and labor organizers as university
students and educated theorists.

One of these murders, the killing with *chiave inglese* of
a young Neo-Fascist named Sergio Ramelli, was particularly brutal and resonated over the years in an unusual
fashion. Ramelli was beaten in the early afternoon of
March 13, 1975; he died of his injuries more than a
month later, on April 29, 1975. That date lies almost
midway between the end of World War II and the present
day; by weird coincidence, Ramelli died the day after the
thirtieth anniversary of the execution by firing squad (by
a partisan platoon) of Benito Mussolini. For several years
running, both dates became occasions for killings and
rioting in Milan. Then, a decade later, one of the killers
shared his feelings of regret and guilt over the murder at
a Milanese party, apparently unaware that one of his
fellow party-goers was a prosecuting magistrate. The trial
that ensued was a weird window into the past. Perhaps
the most disturbing thing was the "archive" that was
found in a Milanese apartment: detailed files on thousands of right-wing activists, with photographs, names of
family members, home addresses, identifying details
(moles, sideburns, etc.). Some of the files were
preprinted forms, carefully filled in. And perhaps,
strangest of all, the archive had been updated and
enlarged over the years. The ten defendants were all doctors; after all, the *servizio d'ordine* (disciplinary squad)
that killed Ramelli was the *servizio d'ordine di Medicina*—

the medical school disciplinary squad. One of the defendants told the court that, over the years, he had found himself unconsciously calling his son, born years afterward, "Sergio."

It was as if the revelations from the Sergio Ramelli case had redefined the national Zeitgeist (or, as some suspected, with a bit more malice, prosecuting magistrates and police investigators had noticed that publicity and promotions might well await those who unearthed old unsolved crimes and brought the perpetrators to justice). A year after the guilty verdict for the killing of Ramelli, a chain of events occurred that cast a bright spotlight back in time, onto some very dark doings, while illuminating much about the current state of Italian law and justice. And, as is the case everywhere on earth, but with seemingly greater intensity in Italy, where there is bright light, there are also dark and all-inclusive shadows.

The incident in question traced its roots back to one of the great cyclonic low-pressure systems of Italy's stormy postwar political history: the bombing of Piazza Fontana in December 1969. An Italian author, Carlo Emilio Gadda, wrote, in his 1957 novel *That Awful Mess on the Via Merulana* (English translation by William Weaver):

> In his wisdom and . . . poverty, Officer Ingravallo
> . . . sustained, among other things, that unforeseen
> catastrophes are never the consequence or the
> effect, if you prefer, of a single motive, of *a* cause
> singular; but that they are rather like a whirlpool,
> a cyclonic point of depression in the consciousness
> of the world, towards which a whole multitude of

converging causes have contributed. He also used words like knot or tangle, or muddle, or *gnommero*, which in Roman dialect means skein. . . . The apparent motive, the principal motive was, of course, single. But the crime was the effect of a whole list of motives which had blown on it in a whirlwind (like the sixteen winds in the list of winds when they twist together in a tornado, in a cyclonic depression) and had ended by pressing into the vortex of the crime the enfeebled "reason of the world."

This is one of the great theoretical enunciations of the way things work in Italy, at every level—fractally—from personal interactions to political and historical movements. This concept, of the turbulent, murky, incestuous nature of all huge and unexpected disasters, can be twinned with the classic statement of the nature of change in Italy, from Giuseppe Tomasi di Lampedusa's *The Leopard*: "If we want things to stay as they are, things will have to change." And just to round out the recipe, former prime minister (and alleged mafioso) Giulio Andreotti's adage: "Power wears down the powerless."

The "unforeseen catastrophe" in question was a bombing in a bank in Milan's Piazza Fontana in December 1969. This event loomed large in the mental geography of Italian extremists. The event in itself was horrifying, but its ripple effects, in the form of arrests, indictments, trials, and miscarriages of justice, amounted to scientific—or, as Giorgio would put it, political—proof of the malevolent duplicity of the Italian government.

The bomb went off late in the afternoon of December 12, 1969. The timing was important in many ways. Logistically, it was clearly timed to cause the maximum number of deaths and injuries: this was a terror strike, not a warning or a message. The site of the bombing, generally known and referred to as Piazza Fontana, was in fact in the main lobby of the Banca Nazionale di Agricoltura. It lay in the heart of the city of Milan, just a few hundred yards from the city's signature cathedral bristling with ornate Gothic spires; but it was a farmer's bank, and Friday afternoon was an especially busy time for the bank. Friday was a market day, and many farmers did their after-market transactions late in the afternoon before heading back out of town. There were also many ordinary city dwellers who had accounts at the bank.

Strategically, it came in the wake of two years of political turmoil in Italy: 1967 was the year of the "hot summer" of labor unrest; 1968 was the year of student protest, which focused on economic issues (in contrast with the American protest movement, largely antiwar). If we are interested in looking at some of the other winds that converged in this cyclonic depression, we would have to look a little farther back. In the early and mid-1960s, in the wake of attempts by the new center-left coalition to promote social and economic reforms, there was some frightening "saber rattling" on the part of right-wing reactionary forces. The term "saber rattling" had been used by the deputy prime minister, the Socialist Pietro Nenni, to describe the reaction to the proposed nationalization of the Italian telephone and electrical systems; the term is abstract, but one of the concrete forms that it took, evident throughout the country, was a massive deployment of military convoys. Everywhere, on local highways and on Italy's massive new superhighways, long convoys of green army trucks rumbled to and fro. They were headed nowhere in particular but they launched a clear warning.

There was more. It emerged a few years later that a military plan, code-named Solo, called for the simultaneous arrest of hundreds if not thousands of suspicious individuals (many of them high officials in left-wing political parties) and their deportation to a "concentration" area on the island of Sardinia. In those years, at times of particular political tension, officials of the Communist and Socialist Parties were often warned not to sleep at home (Italy being Italy, it doesn't take a lot of imagination to picture the secondary uses to which these warnings were put). Although some of the details of this Solo Plan emerged in the mid-sixties, further links to a NATO "stay-behind" army, code-named Gladio, were not to emerge until the 1990s.

And to put things into context: the right-wing military takeover of neighboring Greece in 1967 was viewed in Italy as a clear warning of what awaited excessively reform-minded nations.

The bombing, then. A leather briefcase, loaded with high explosives and timers, was left under a heavy marble counter in the bank lobby. The blast killed sixteen and wounded eighty-eight. In the aftermath of the explosion, as the dust cleared and after the dead, dying, and injured had all been taken away, a photographer took an eloquent picture: a collection of dusty, crumpled hats piled on a bank counter.

Three other bombs went off virtually simultaneously in Rome. One wounded thirteen in a bank; two others went off on the Altar to the Fatherland, a giant neo-rococo monument known popularly as the "wedding cake." A fifth bomb, which failed to explode, was found not far from Piazza Fontana in Milan; the police blew it up hours later, and thus eradicated any evidence that might have been present (and, to be fair, possibly ensured investigators' safety).

Five sets of indictments, eight trials, and three major investigative paths later, it would appear now that right-wing neo-Fascist terrorists of the group Ordine Nuovo (literally, New Order) were responsible for the Piazza Fontana bombing (and the verdict in the latest trial was handed down in the summer of 2001, fully thirty-two years after the murderous attack). At the time, however, the investigators set out in full cry after left-wing suspects. In a "counterinvestigation" of the bombing of Piazza Fontana, the extraparliamentarian group Lotta Continua reported that an investigating magistrate in the nearby Palace of Justice had heard the sound of the bomb going off. A colleague allegedly said to him, "That was probably a boiler exploding"—a fairly common occurrence in Milan in the late sixties. He is alleged to have replied, "I think that was a bomb, and it sounded like an anarchist bomb to me." The investigating magistrate had the waspish personality of a real-life Javert: once, after a fellow magistrate offered him a ride home, the generous driver is said to have received in the mail a few days later a fine for speeding. But if he was a Javert, the state was behind him. The official theory on the bombing for years thereafter was that it had been a left-wing, possibly an anarchist bomb. The police arrested an anarchist the same day, Giuseppe Pinelli, a railroad employee and decidedly not a violent extremist. He was held and interrogated, illegally, for three days without a lawyer. Then, on the evening of December 15, Giuseppe Pinelli flew—or slithered, according to one eyewitness—out of the fifth-floor window of Detective Luigi Calabresi's office. The question of whether he slithered or arced out over the courtyard as he fell became a crucial piece of evidence. The official police line was that Pinelli had collapsed under questioning. Evidently prodded by a guilty conscience, he cried, "This spells the end of anarchy!" and hurled himself out the window. He died a few hours later in the hospital, without recovering consciousness.

A newly founded extraparliamentary organization, Lotta Continua (Continuous Struggle), undertook what it termed a counterinvestigation, and at the time published information that pointed to the most likely suspects (legal proceedings are still under way in Italy against Delfo Zorzi, among others; clearly, the bombing was the work of right-wing extremists); Lotta Continua also called for "proletarian justice" against Detective Calabresi.

From the point of view of someone like Giorgio, here is how things looked. The president of the Italian Chamber of Deputies, Sandro Pertini, attended the funeral ceremonies for the victims of the bombing of

Piazza Fontana. Pertini was one of those rarest of figures, a universally beloved and respected Italian military hero. He had been one of the leaders of the Italian Resistance, and he officially declared the liberation of the city of Milan, making him the Italian equivalent of, say, Charles De Gaulle; he remained in politics and, unlike De Gaulle, stayed on the left. After serving as President of the Chamber of Deputies (the rough equivalent in the Italian Parliament of the House Majority Leader in the United States), he became the president of the Italian Republic. At the funeral ceremonies in December 1969, he is said to have refused to shake the hand of the chief of police of Milan, Marcello Guida, the same man who announced the death of Pinelli. The reason was simple: Pertini had been imprisoned under Mussolini as an anti-Fascist activist on the island of Ventotene. The warden of the Fascist political prison had been none other than Marcello Guida.

It was popular among American antiwar activists to call the police and other high government officials Fascists; in Italy, the expression was literally applicable. More even than in post-Nazi Germany, where a fair portion of the administrative infrastructure had been preserved intact (bureaucracy, judiciary, police, military), in Italy something like 60 percent of the Fascist administrative personnel kept their jobs and careers. General Mark Clark, who oversaw the Allied occupation of Italy, is said to have commented wryly that the greatest disappearing act in history had been that of 40 million Italian Fascists. That may not be entirely fair (Italy had a very respectable Resistance movement), as somebody did have to run the country, yet the point remains that not only were the partisans a source of inspiration for someone like Giorgio but also the people whom the partisans had fought were still, arguably, firmly in power.

So when the former warden of a Fascist political prison, now the police chief of Milan, announced that a guilt-tormented anarchist had killed himself during questioning, skepticism was the general response. Evidence emerged soon enough that pointed to New Order right-wing terrorists from the northern, German-speaking fringe regions of Italy; the prosecuting magistrate finally cobbled together an indictment grouping neo-Nazis defendants with an anarchist (a ballet dancer named Pietro Valpreda), one of the more unlikely conspiracies imaginable. (Though, it must be said, one of the most extreme and questionable militant groups operating in this time of turmoil actually called itself the Nazi-Maoists; this odd syncretic grouping was, however, thought to conceal the hand of the Italian secret services, always eager to infiltrate and even encourage extremist groups.)

In any case, there was now a political price on the head of Detective Luigi Calabresi, the man thought to be responsible for Pinelli's death and for helping to cover up the investigation of the Piazza Fontana bombing. Dario Fo, the Nobel laureate and actor, made his reputation with his play, *Accidental Death of an Anarchist*, based on Pinelli's killing. Evidence continued to emerge. The one nonpolice witness to Pinelli's fall, a journalist for the Communist daily paper, *L'Unità*, testified that he had heard three thumps—two as Pinelli hit narrow cornices along the wall on the way down, a third when he hit the floor of the courtyard. And yet a postmortem examination showed absolutely no abrasions on Pinelli's hands; he had not made even instinctive efforts to ward off the onrushing obstacles. The journalist noted the time, and reported it as three minutes after midnight. The police, in the days that followed, revised that time slightly back, to three minutes before midnight. The reason soon became clear: an emergency call had been made to the hospital at that time, and a special timing device on the hospital's switchboard had recorded the time. Perhaps the emergency call had been made before the anarchist flew from the window. The doctors in the emergency room noted that, even though Pinelli's head had absorbed the final impact, there was no bleeding from nose and mouth. Could Pinelli have been dead before he was thrown from the window? The policemen present in the room at the time changed their story more than once. They said, first, that Pinelli had rushed to the window and leapt out; then, that they had tried to restrain him by grabbing at his clothing, which would explain why he slid down the wall instead of arcing out over the courtyard; and, in the third of three versions, that one of the policemen had actually succeeded in seizing Pinelli's shoe, which came off in his hand as Pinelli fell. This led to the absurdity of three shoes. All of the journalists who rushed out into the courtyard minutes later agreed: the dying (or dead) Pinelli's feet had been fully shod.

The anarchist's widow, Licia Pinelli, brought a civil suit against Calabresi for the wrongful death of her husband. A verdict was handed down in 1975, finding that Pinelli had suffered an "active seizure" (a term not found in medical books) and that Calabresi was innocent of his death. In any case, it was too late.

At 9:15 on the morning of May 17, 1972, Luigi Calabresi was killed as he left the street door of his apartment building, with a single bullet to the head. This was the first left-wing political assassination in what would come to be called the Years of Lead. A number of leads were followed, on the left and on the right. Finally the investigators called it quits, and it remained one of the great topics of conversation in post–Years of Lead Milan and Italy at large: who had killed Calabresi?

An answer—almost certainly not *the* answer—came sixteen years later, in the slow churning of the Italian judicial system. As so often seems to be the case, the result was a Fellini-esque pastiche of the weird and the unlikely, the sinister and the patently absurd. In the late summer of 1988, in a beach town along the Tyrrhenian Coast of Italy, a crepe vendor named Leonardo Marino entered an office of the Carabinieri, Italy's paramilitary police force, and stated that he wished to confess to involvement in an old and unsolved crime. According to the official police minutes of his interview, he would not specify what crime, or when and where it had been committed. And yet very high-level Carabinieri veterans of the antiterrorism division were immediately alerted. One in particular traveled the two hundred miles to the coast to speak with Marino, who was then taken to Milan for further questioning.

After several days, Marino named names: Giorgio

Pietrostefani, Ovidio Bompressi, and Adriano Sofri (Sofri was the showstopper; the founder and former chief of Lotta Continua, he was now an adviser to the powerful Italian Socialist Party). Marino also specified the crime: the murder of Luigi Calabresi.

There ensued a succession of trials and appeals trials and Supreme Court reviews to rival Piazza Fontana. The final outcome was sentences of twenty-two years in prison for each of the defendants, and absolution for Marino. The chief problem with the prosecution's case was that it rested entirely on the confession of Leonardo Marino, and that confession was riddled with inconsistencies.

Among the most important of these inconsistencies, Marino, in what sounded suspiciously like a coached statement, told the court that, tormented by the pangs of conscience, he had turned himself in to the Carabinieri in a spontaneous act of contrition (his exact words in Italian were roughly this stilted). In fact, through various threads of testimony and cross-examination, it became clear that Marino had been talking to the Carabinieri in regular nighttime meetings, for as long as six weeks prior to the supposed date of his confession. There is no record of these conversations, and no one has ever explained what was discussed. It is known that Marino was an old friend of both Adriano Sofri—a major intellectual figure on the Italian left—and of Giorgio Pietrostefani, another leader of Lotta Continua. In fact, Marino's two sons are named Adriano and Giorgio. It is also known that Marino was having serious financial difficulties prior to his "spontanous confession," and that the last time he had seen Sofri was to ask for a loan of 20 million lire, a loan that was refused.

The other problems with Marino's testimony are too numerous to list here in their entirety, but some of the biggest howlers are worth noting. And remember, the entire prosecution case against the three is based exclusively on Marino's testimony.

Marino described the crucial meeting at Pisa, on May 13, 1972, in which Adriano Sofri is said to have ordered the killing. It was a day of demonstrations in response to the police killing of a young anarchist, Franco Serantini. Sofri addressed the crowd; after the demonstration, according to Marino, they had a conversation in which Sofri confirmed that the order had been given by the executive commission of Lotta Continua.

It would almost be comical to trace the evolution of Marino's account of this conversation, if it had not been used as the basis for three prison sentences of twenty-two years each. In his first description of events, Marino recalled that Sofri and Pietrostefani had both been present and that they had spoken with him immediately after the speeches, alone. It then emerged that Pietrostefani at the time was wanted by the police for questioning; it would have been the height of folly for him to attend a demonstration under heavy police surveillance. Obligingly, Marino changed his recollection: Pietrostefani had only spoken to him on the phone a few days previous; he had spoken to Sofri alone. They spoke on the street. Only then did it emerge that in Marino's account there was no mention of the pouring rain that all the other attendees recalled. In time this too was taken into account. Marino said that they had stood out in the rain for perhaps ten minutes, and as questioning went on, that time was reduced even more, to a few minutes. A few minutes in which he discussed an order to commit a murder, his own misgivings, Sofri's reassurances, and all the steps that would be taken to take care of Marino's family.

There are other problems with the testimony. It would appear that there was an accident, the morning of the killing, in a parking lot nearby; it had long been thought that one of the cars involved in the accident was the getaway car, used by the killers just a few minutes later. Marino willingly described this accident in specific detail and testified that in fact it had been he driving the getaway car and that he had fled the scene of the accident. His account differed sharply from the accounts of the other driver, both as given at the time and almost two decades later in court. The judge's evalutation of this discrepancy: clearly, the eyewitness was mistaken, since Marino had actually been there.

This Procrustean approach to evidence and testimony extended to the treatment of the evidence. The car used by the murderers, abandoned in a nearby square and impounded by the state, was actually demolished *after* the case was reopened. A disappointing mistake, because it made it impossible to verify Marino's description of how he had forced the wind wing in order to steal the car. In any case, though, the forensic records would seem to contradict his account.

It is, I suppose, possible that Marino just wasn't good on details; I covered the first of the numerous Calabresi murder trials, and I recall that Marino's account was compelling, particularly his description of Ovidio Bompressi, the accused gunman, getting into the getaway car driven by Marino after the shooting, and saying, only, "What a mess." (And a mess it was; photographs of the scene depict a pool of blood, and the car door was splattered with brains.)

But Marino's account systematically conflicts with the descriptions given immediately after the events. Where they clash, it is assumed that the eyewitness accounts were mistaken, because Marino had actually been there, and we have his confession as proof.

Perhaps it is this, above all else, that is worth noting in the history of political crime in Italy and the trials for those crimes: a succession of ambiguity, missteps, and unlikely evidence.

To take an example from our own political life: it has been argued, convincingly, that the Warren Commission hedged the details of Lee Harvey Oswald's Russian connections—meaningless connections ultimately (the KGB father-in-law was a minor provincial official; the defection and repatriation were simply the ping-ponging frenzy of a misfit megalomaniac seeking a place in which to be important)—out of fear that the connections would in fact be inflammatory in a time of extreme Cold War tension. That seems like a plausible explanation for much of what is wrong with the Warren Commission Report; it hedged the truth for contingent political considerations. And yet in so hedging, it generated a massive and paranoid distrust among America's left-wing antiwar activists, and later on the right as well. Once you start editing the truth in judicial investigations, it is hard to tell what the result will be. The Warren Commission Report, plus lots and lots of mind-altering drugs consumed on epidemic levels, combined with a few movies by Oliver Stone, equals a truly paranoid mind-set on a mass level. Italy had dozens and dozens of Warren Commission Reports (there is actually a parliamentary commission, the Commissione Stragi, charged with investigating the string of "massacres" that are also referred to by the popular press as the "Misteri d'Italia," or the "mysteries of Italy"), plenty of drugs, and political groups ranging from Nazi-Maoists to actual Fascists— real live Fascists who had spent time with Mussolini— and of course, the CIA.

To draw a line from the Warren Commission Report to the Weather Underground, the Symbionese Liberation Army, or Timothy McVeigh is silly on the face of it.

And yet, and yet. An Italian author—a Sicilian author, to be precise—now dead, Leonardo Sciascia wrote in an editorial in the *Corriere della Sera*, on January 10, 1987, that the fact that an investigating magistrate in Sicily, Paolo Borsellino, should have been promoted to a position of greater responsibility specifically because of his involvement in Mafia trials, is something that should give pause. In this editorial, Sciascia wrote that the worrisome lesson to be drawn from this preferential promotion is the following: in Sicily today (that is, fifteen years ago), there is a career to be made by being a member of the "antimafia." Sciascia's point is a subtle one, and he buttresses it with an account of the efforts of the prefect Cesare Mori in the 1920s. Mori was sent by Mussolini to uproot the Mafia; known as the Iron Prefect, Mori used the methods of an Indian fighter. He took women and children hostage, he rooted out the small-time rural Mafiosi, and he relied upon the cooperation of powerful and corrupt landowners of the area. The local Mafia was officially suppressed, but as soon as it could be reimported in a new and virulent form from the United States, in the wake of the invading American forces, it flourished again with unabated vigor. Sciascia's point is this: it is of very little value to suppress a sociological phenomenon like the Mafia, which has deep and widespread roots in the populace at large, in anything other than a truly democratic fashion, with the administration of true justice. Simple repression can only be a stopgap. Sciascia cites (elsewhere, for other purposes, but it serves perfectly as an illustration) the case of Don Vito Cascio-Ferro, a major figure in the Black Hand of New York around the turn of the twentieth century, who was said to have been responsible for the killing in Palermo of the New York detective, Joe Petrosino. Don Vito continued to run a transatlantic operation, largely from Palermo, until Mori and the Fascists arrested him for a murder, that of a certain Gioacchino Lo Voi. The evidence was insufficient, but Mori succeeded in cooking up false evidence, upon which the defendant was convicted and sentenced to life imprisonment. Don Vito is said to have exclaimed in court that, with all the murders he had committed and for which they had been unable to convict him, he was being convicted of a murder that he had not committed.

This is not an insubstantial point. One of the foundations of the Mafia's survival is very basic; it provides protection and a rudimentary if quick form of justice. One prosecutor in southern Italy explained it to me in this way: If you sue someone in an Italian court of justice, much less in a southern Italian court of justice, you might win a judgment in eight or nine years; and even then, it would be practically impossible to secure compensation. If, on the other hand, you go to the local enforcer, you will have quick and effective recourse, albeit with a sizable payoff to the mob.

If the state goes in to uproot a rudimentary system of social justice using the methods typically used to repress a guerrilla uprising, the result will not be a stable system of justice, but a precarious and temporary system imposed from without.

For these observations, Sciascia was branded as a member of the anti-antimafia, an apologist for the Mafia. The debate, amplified and rendered even more hysterical in the Italian press, left Sciascia with the reputation of supporting the Sicilian Mafia, a completely unfair slander.

Sciascia wrote a series of editorials in the weeks that followed, attempting to reiterate his position. At one point, he seems resigned to the hurricane of criticism that was directed at him: "There are those who may know how to write, and who in fact, write well and publish the things that they write in newspapers, but who are absolutely incapable of reading, and understanding what they read."

It sounds almost like the voice of Giorgio—sarcastic, biting, and infinitely patient, as if in proportion to the amount of patience required.

The fight against the Mafia was necessarily closely related to the fight against terrorism; indeed, it was almost a direct result. One figure in particular provides the link: Carabiniere General Carlo Alberto Dalla Chiesa.

Dalla Chiesa is an interesting figure—widely beloved as a martyred Mafia-fighting folk hero among the middle class of Italy, with a fringe of die-hard radicals who still revile him for his work in defeating the terrorists. Dalla Chiesa emerged from the Carabinieri, an unusual corps among the various Italian police forces. They are generally referred to in English-language news reporting as a paramilitary police force, without much more explanation than that. They are in fact part of the Italian army (hence the possibility of the rank of Carabiniere General), and they therefore operate with a certain degree of independence from some of the political administrative strictures binding other Italian police forces; they come under the supervision of the Ministry of Defense, not the Ministry of the Interior (which oversees other police corps) or the Ministry of Justice. They are in a sense a holdover from a time when Italy was an artificial construction, a cluster of statelings and principalities assembled into a theoretical nation in the late nineteenth century (not coincidentally, at the same time as Germany, in 1870) by liberal, progressive, capitalist forces from the north. The first capital of the new Italy was Turin, and the Carabinieri were deployed all over the peninsula and the several islands, almost as an occupying military force. They have a grim origin, at least in the lore and legend of Italy. The story that most Italians can tell you is that in the early years of the Italian army, the Carabinieri, with their eponymous carbine rifles, were positioned in the rear, to shoot any retreating would-be deserters. This weaselly and fearsome original reputation declined into a more agreeable if still dismissive icon—as the butt of jokes. What Polish jokes were in America, and what the Belgians were to the French, the Carabinieri were to Italians: Why is Carabinieri written on the side doors of their squad cars? If it were written on the back, they'd try to get in the trunk . . . and so on.

But the Carabinieri were an effective force, and under Dalla Chiesa, and with American assistance, they succeeded in dismantling much of the terrorist infrastructure in the course of the last few years of the 1970s and the first years of the 1980s. Imagine the grim confirmation of Giorgio's worldview with the next act of the drama. With the growing problem of the Mafia in Sicily, Dalla Chiesa agreed to take on the Mafia, in the wake of a bloody mob war that had also resulted in the killings of high-level Sicilian politicians. He spent a hundred days in Palermo, capital of Sicily, and after a couple of months, in August 1982, he gave an interview to the distinguished Italian journalist Giorgio Bocca in which he openly said that he felt he was completely isolated, that no one was watching his back. He had requested special investigative powers; he never received them. His objective was the banks. Although the Sicilian economy was anemic at best, bank branches had been opening on the island at record rates. Clearly, money was being laundered; it was all part of a triangle in which raw opium was brought into Sicily from Turkey and points east, refined into heroin, shipped to New York and points west in exchange for cash and weapons (which were then shipped back east in exchange for more opium). There was a constant surplus flow of cash, however, and the banks were there to process it.

Proof of government connivance is tenuous, but as Pier Paolo Pasolini put it, "I know. But I have no proof. I don't even have any evidence." There is a simple equation: take on the terrorists, and become a hero. Take on the Mafia, and suddenly you are alone, and you die. Carabiniere General Carlo Alberto Dalla Chiesa took on the Mafia and on September 3, 1982, as he drove in the streets of Palermo with his young wife and a bodyguard in a small car, with no armor plating, he was killed by a hail of bullets from a Kalashnikov assault rifle.

His successors took greater care. Giovanni Falcone, a great anti-Mafia investigator and prosecutor, once wrote that in Palermo the expression goes: "To prove that you are honest, you must die." He traveled in heavily armor-plated vehicles, but even that was not enough. In May 1992, the Mafia killed him on his way into the city of Palermo from the airport of Punta Raisi; he was traveling in a convoy of three cars. Over two thousand pounds of high explosives were detonated in a pedestrian underpass beneath the superhighway and blasted open a crater a hundred feet wide and twenty-five feet deep. The explosion sent the first car with three bodyguards pinwheeling into a nearby olive grove and split in two the car with Falcone, his magistrate wife, and a fourth bodyguard. Only the two bodyguards in the third car survived. Less than two months later, the Mafia struck again, killing an investigating magistrate named Paolo

Borsellino (the anti-Mafia magistrate about whom Sciascia had written his controversial editorial).

And so to someone like Giorgio, there must have been little doubt about who had won the war, and just which group was allied with which.

Other choice links existed between the Mafia and the Italian government, some of which were surely known to Giorgio when he wrote his *Memoirs,* and some of which he could only intuit: During the fifty-five-day captivity of former Italian prime minister and Christian Democratic leader Aldo Moro, kidnapped and ultimately executed by the Red Brigades in 1978, the Christian Democratic party is known to have reached out to contacts in the underworld of organized crime at least in two directions—to imprisoned mob boss Raffaele Cutolo, head of the NCO, or New Organized Camorra (there are three distinct major criminal organizations in Southern Italy: the Mafia in Sicily; the 'ndrangheta in Calabria, at the toe of the Italian boot; and a little further up the western, Tyrrhenian coast, the Camorra of Naples); and the Banda della Magliana, a Rome-based criminal organization. Neither of these leads worked, assuming that there had been any real intention of saving Moro (the Moro kidnapping, in a sense the Ur-text of all the "Mysteries of Italy"), but the stunning imagery of high government officials reaching out to the underworld for help in solving a crime so *everything can return to an orderly state* is worthy of a scene from Fritz Lang's *M.*

A few years later, the Red Brigades kidnapped and held for ransom a Christian Democratic parliamentarian named Ciro Cirillo. Once again, the Christian Democrats reached out to Don Raffaele Cutolo. This time, the mediation was successful.

There was no love lost, however, between Mafia and left-wing extremists. By and large, they left each other alone, but their basic views clashed. One of the most eloquent clashes in ideology occurred in 1988, when Mauro Rostagno, a former leader in Lotta Continua and a graduate of the same northeastern Italian school of sociology (Trent) that produced many of the leaders of the Red Brigades, decided to go to southwestern Sicily and set up a center for recovering drug addicts. He stumbled upon a little-covered section of the Sicilian drug-trading Mafia and, on a local public-access television station, he preached what amounted to secular sermons against it, real barn-burning stem-winders, with all the venom and urgency and ineluctable logic of the most heated leftist speechifying of the Years of Lead. The videos still exist, and they are amazing. The vehemence and aggressivity with which Rostagno attacked the local Mafia druglord is frightening to see, especially for a viewer who knows what comes afterward. For Rostagno died in the proverbial hail of bullets as he pulled up to the driveway of his rural detox center. It turned out that there had been a mysterious blackout, reported by a technician of the rural power company. Eight years later it emerged that the same technician was also the personal driver of Vincenzo Virga, the local drug boss.

And even between the traditionally friendly Christian Democratic Party and the Cosa Nostra, there were fallings-out. The Christian Democratic Party, which, much like the Italian Communist Party, no longer exists (the new names are, respectively, the Popular Party and the Party of the United Left), was embodied by one person in particular—the dry-witted, patient, infinitely sinister Giulio Andreotti, whose physical appearance has been nicely described by Richard Drake in his valuable *The Aldo Moro Murder Case*: "The exceedingly familiar face, inscrutable and bespectacled, had changed little after forty years of public life. A slight hump on his back and two rather large turned-out ears remained the delight and inspiration of political cartoonists." Other features of Andreotti's appearance are his thick, square-lensed, plastic-framed eyeglasses and his patient calculating demeanor. One of the more memorable photographs of the Honorable Andreotti—seven times prime minister, repeatedly cabinet-level minister, now senator for life—shows him seated at his desk in Parliament. The picture is taken from above, and reveals his black, neatly combed hair, his plastic eyeglass frames, his dark pinstriped suit over his slightly bulging hunched back, and his arms curving over the desk with his hands lightly touching, the fingers arced out in an intricate web of patient calculation. His nickname, originally in deadly earnest on the Italian left and eventually—jocularly—throughout Italian society, is Beelzebub. He is currently on trial for involvement in the Mafia; he has been tried and acquitted several times already for charges ranging from Mafia conspiracy to actual conspiracy in the mysterious death of an exceedingly mysterious journalist (named Mino Pecorelli, who deserves a book all on his own). The former Socialist leader and prime minister Bettino Craxi said of Andreotti: "He is a fox, but all foxes eventually wind up being made into fur coats." Craxi died in exile in Algeria. So far no one has succeeded in tanning Andreotti's pelt.

Even between the Christian Democrats and the Mafia, then, things turned cranky. And it was astonishing when it finally happened. There is reason to think that every leftist's suspicion of the way things work in a capitalist democracy was fully justified by Andreotti's special interest in Sicily. For that was the long-lived Christian Democratic veteran's electoral power base, because the Mafia controlled—perhaps still controls—votes, thousands and thousands of votes. Like a powerful union officer (think Johnny Friendly or the UAW, as you prefer) or the CEO of Boeing in Seattle—or perhaps more pertinently, the CEO of Fiat in Turin—Sicily was one huge company town, and the company in question was the Mafia. Andreotti's point man in Sicily was named Salvo Lima, and although nothing has been proven ("I have no proof. I don't even have any evidence"), we do know that, as the pressure ratcheted up in the early nineties, as the state finally bore down on the Mafia, and as the mass media focused an increasingly hostile glare on the old comfortable relationships, Salvo Lima one morning was chased from his bulletproof car and shot down like a dog on the sidewalk (March 1992). There are those who conjecture that Andreotti must have turned down some excessively insistent requests for favors or cover. But, again, there is no proof.

There is much more to be said about Giorgio's worldview, and indeed the world in which he lived (in so many ways, Italy of twenty years ago is more distant than the United States, or France, or the U.K. at that time, though perhaps not quite as distant as Spain or China or Russia in the 1980s), but I would like to try to reach far- ther into the past for what is perhaps the darkest chapter of them all, and yet the most enlightening. At the very foundation of the Italian state, the state against which Giorgio was leveling his gun in what he hoped would be an act useful to others, lies a chapter of brutish nihilism that explains a great deal. Giorgio wrote: "I like a world where something rustles in the dark, where there's some- thing out there, but it's too soon to tell what it is." A largely forgotten chapter of Italian history rustles in the nation's dark; perhaps Giorgio recalled it occasionally in his ruminations.

When Italy was assembled as a state, in 1870, one of the most reluctant component parts was the Kingdom of the Two Sicilies, comprising all the southern lands now possessed of their own indigenous structures of organ- ized crime. Perhaps it should be referred to as the Kingdom of the Mafia, the 'ndrangheta, and the Camorra. The Kingdom of the Two Sicilies was ruled by a branch of the Bourbon dynasty that also ruled in France and Spain, and for a number of years southern Italy was riven by a reaction known as the Brigand Wars.

Brigand armies, sometimes thousands-strong, fought against the occupying northern Italian troops. What they wanted is not clear, but that they did not want to be part of a modern, liberal, tax-paying state was certainly clear.

The new unified Italian state was afraid of appearing weak and unstable, and it reacted harshly. Generals destroyed entire towns that had greeted the brigands. To give a sense of what was facing the 120,000 northern troops, there were 388 "verified brigand bands," each with anywhere from 5 to 15 persons, up to as many as 100. In the four most intense years of conflict, 13,583 brigands were "eliminated" (July 1861 to December 1865).

The rest of Europe was appalled, no matter how decisive the Italian reaction may have been. There was a wholesale slaughter of civilians going on, second only— as one writer observed—to the slaughter of Indians in the United States.

And once the repression of the brigandage was complete, which only happened twenty years after the initial outbreak, in 1880, people began leaving, crossing the Atlantic in search of their fortunes elsewhere. Giustino Fortunato, a nineteenth-century Italian parliamentarian who was the standard-bearer of the southern movement in Italy, pinpointed the painful link between the suppression of brigandage and the great transoceanic emigration that followed, describing them both as phases in a great rural peasant secession from the Italian state. As Italian statesman Francesco Saverio Nitti put it: "Either brigand or emigrant."

It is perhaps romanticizing to call the brigands anarchist heroes *avant la lettre*. After all, one brigand chief wrote to a family whose children he had kidnapped and was holding for a ransom that was not immediately forthcoming: "Signori, we send you these ears because we have heard that you are poor. And so we send you meat so that you can make a little soup to eat." Cynics, sadists, even psychopaths. And yet, in the hardscrabble, unlettered south, the brigands were the only ones who were standing up to the new and bewildering government.

Let me quote at some length from Carlo Levi's *Christ Stopped at Eboli*:

> Governments, Theocracies, and Armies are, of course, stronger than the scattered peasants. So the peasants have to resign themselves to being dominated, but they cannot feel as their own the glories and undertakings of a civilization that is radically their enemy. The only wars that touch their hearts are those in which they have fought to defend themselves against that civilization, against History and Government, Theocracy and the Army. These wars they fought under their own black pennants, without military leadership or training and without hope, ill-fated wars that they were bound to lose, fierce and desperate wars, incomprehensible to historians.
>
> The peasants of Gagliano were indifferent to the conquest of Abyssinia and they neither remembered the World War nor spoke of its dead, but one war was close to their hearts and constantly on their tongues; it was already a fable, a legend, a myth, an epic story. This was the war of the brigands. Brigandage had come to an end in 1865, seventy years before, and only a very few of them were old enough to remember it, either as participants or eye witnesses. But all of them, old and young, men and women, spoke of it with as much passion as if it

were only yesterday. When I talked to the peasants I could be sure that, whatever was the subject of our conversation, we should in one way or another slip into mention of the brigands. Their traces are everywhere; there is not a mountain, gully, wood, fountain, cave, or stone that is not linked with one of their adventures or that did not serve them as a refuge or hide-out; not a dark corner that was not their meeting-place; not a country chapel where they did not leave threatening letters or wait for ransom money. Many places, like the Fossa del Bersagliere, were named for their deeds. . . .

The myth of the brigands is close to their hearts and a part of their lives, the only poetry in their existence, their dark, desperate epic. Even the appearance of the peasants today recalls that of the brigands: they are silent, lonely, gloomy and frowning in their black suits and hats and, in winter, black overcoats, armed whenever they set out for the fields with gun and axe. They have gentle hearts and patient souls; centuries of resignation weigh on their shoulders, together with a feeling of the vanity of all things and of the overbearing power of fate. But when, after infinite endurance, they are shaken to the depths of their beings and are driven by an instinct of self-defence or justice, their revolt knows no bounds and no measure. It is an unhuman revolt whose point of departure and final end alike are death, in which ferocity is born of despair. The brigands unreasonably and hopelessly stood up for the life and liberty of the peasants against the encroachments of the State. By ill luck they were unwitting instruments of History; they were on the wrong side and they came to destruction. But through the brigands the peasants defended themselves against the hostile civilization that never understands but everlastingly enslaves them; instinctively they looked on the brigands as heroes. . . .

There should be a history of this Italy, a history outside the framework of time, confining itself to that which is changeless and eternal, in other words, a mythology. This Italy has gone its way in darkness and silence, like the earth, in a sequence of recurrent seasons and recurrent misadventures. . . .

The fourth national war of the peasants was brigandage and here, too, the humble Italy was historically on the wrong side and bound to lose. The brigands had neither the arms forged by Vulcan nor the heavy artillery of the government troops. Even their gods were powerless: of what avail was a poor Madonna with a black face against the Ethical state of the Neapolitan followers of Hegel? Brigandage was an access of heroic folly and desperate savagery, a desire for wreaking death and ruin, with no hope of final victory. "If the world had only one enormous heart, I'd tear it out," said Caruso, one of the most fearful brigand chiefs.

This blind urge to destruction, this bloody and suicidal will to annihilation, has lurked for centuries beneath the patient endurance of daily toil. Every revolt on the part of the peasants springs out of an elementary desire for justice deep at the dark bottom of their hearts. After the end of brigandage, this land sank into an uneasy peace. But every now and then in some village or other, when the peasants have no representation in the government and defence in the law, they rise up with death in their hearts, burn the town hall or the barracks of the *Carabinieri*, kill the gentry, and then go off in silent resignation to prison. . . .

If the brigands cut off the ears, nose, and tongue of the gentry in order to obtain a ransom, the soldiers, in their turn, cut off the heads of the brigands they caught and mounted them on poles in the village as an example. Thus the war of destruction went on. These clay mountains are studded with holes and natural caves. Here the brigands lay low, hiding in the trunks of hollow trees the money obtained from robbery and ransom. When the brigand bands were at last dispersed, their loot remained in the woods. At this point the history of the brigands passes into legend and is bound up with age-old superstitions. For the brigands hid their spoils in the places where the peasants had always imagined there was hidden treasure. In this way the brigands came to be looked upon as beings with the dark powers of the nether regions.

Bloodthirsty they may well have been, but they were being hunted down with a degree of ruthlessness reminiscent of the treatment accorded the Indians in our own American West.

General La Marmora, a hero of the Italian Risorgimento, made the following statement to the parliamentary commission of inquest on brigandage: "From the month of May 1861 to the month of February 1863, we have killed or executed by firing squad 7,151 brigands. I know nothing more, I can say nothing more."

Early in the process of repression, an Italian general issued the following proclamation:

> Major General Commander of the Troops of Further Abbruzzo II Orders that:
> 1) Anyone caught with firearms, knife, blades, or any other weapons for cutting or stabbing, who cannot show authorization by the Established Authorities, will be immediately executed by firing squad.
> 2) Anyone who is shown to have incited the peasants to rebel, by word or payment or other means, will be immediately executed by firing squad.
> 3) The same penalty will be imposed on those who by word or other deed insult the Coat of Arms of the House of Savoy, the portrait of the King, or the national flag of Italy.
>
> General Ferdinando Pinelli

And, if a peasant could be shot by firing squad for carrying a hunting knife, a brigand could become a conquering hero for taking arms against the occupying army.

One of the great brigand chiefs, Carmine Crocco

Donatelli, describes his triumphal welcome by the populace of Melfi, a fair-sized town of almost twenty thousand:

> I was greeted to the sound of music by a deputation of the wealthiest citizens of the city, while the churchbells pealed and chimed, the balconies were crowded with people and draped with colorful tapestries, and women threw flowers and blew kisses . . . on the evening of my arrival there were candlelight processions and parties, balls and riotous drinking. . . .

There are tales of the semispontaneous uprisings that terrified both southern liberals and northern politicians.

On August 7, 1861, in Pontelandalfo, during a religious procession that the whole town attended, at a signal from the priests, the town hall was burned to the ground, the homes of "liberals" were torched, two "gentlemen" were killed, and a new government was formed. It immediately sent out messages to the surrounding towns and urged them to revolt as well.

Fifty sharpshooters (*Bersaglieri*: refer back to the Fossa del Bersagliere from Carlo Levi; *fossa* means ravine, but *fossa del bersagliere* means a *bersagliere*'s grave) from the Italian army arrived four days later. The mob attacked them; part of the platoon took refuge in a tower, but despite the constant gunfire from the soldiers, the mob scaled the tower and killed all the soldiers with stones and pruning hooks. The rest of the soldiers fled to the countryside and entered the town of Casalduni to seek shelter. They were greeted with heavy volleys of rifle fire. Only one survived.

Numerically speaking, that is not so very different from the several hundred dead of Custer's Last Stand; psychologically, to an Italian government unaware that it was at war, it must have been even more shocking.

On August 13, a large force, of roughly regiment strength, of *Bersaglieri* (the 18th Regiment) arrived and found their slaughtered comrades. They burned both towns to the ground. The colonel in command of the regiment telegraphed his commander in Naples: "Justice has been done against Pontelandalfo and Casalduni."

The next day, the armed garrison of the nearby town of Rionero tried to capture Ruvo del Monte, occupied by Crocco. The brigand was quick and skillful. He had dug trenches, and he successfully resisted three massed charges by the Piedmontese occupation troops. They were forced to retreat. That night the brigands celebrated their victory by feasting on a thousand chickens and two hundred sheep.

And there were remarkably devious plots. One of the most noteworthy was described by Leonard Sciascia in a short book entitled *I Pugnalatori* (not translated into English). The title translates as *The Stabbers*, or *The Dagger Wielders*, or *The Knifers*. One evening in the mid-1860s in Palermo, Sicily, eleven men were stabbed, several fatally, within minutes of each other at eleven different places in the city. Charted on a map, the locations of the stabbings formed an eleven-pointed star, all points equidistant from the city center. Only one of the stabbers was caught, but eyewitness accounts of the other ten who fled made it clear that they were dressed identically: low-browed black hat and ample black cape. From the testimony of the one captured knifeman, the police—and especially a Piedmontese investigating magistrate newly arrived in the city from the north—were able to identify and question several other stabbers. Their evidence all pointed to one, unthinkable mastermind: a Bourbon prince, member of the aristocracy of the Two Sicilies, but now an avowedly wholehearted supporter of the Unified Italy and a member of the new Italian parliament. Sicily being Sicily (and for that matter, Italy being Italy), matters were succeessfully covered up, and the Honorable Member of Parliament was acquitted of all responsibility in the stabbings and killings. But the original documents and Sciascia's skillful analysis of the investigation give us a glimpse of an audacious and twisted conspiracy to sow terror and destabilize the established order.

This is one more panoply of crime into which has been pressed, perhaps, the "enfeebled 'reason of the world' "—at least, of Giorgio's world.

So far this troll through the history of Italian state-sponsored, or state-indulged, crime of the postwar era (with a brief voyage farther back, to the post-Risorgimento years) has followed in the tradition of what Jorge Luis Borges once described as a Universal History of Infamy, and the reference to the Argentine author is no accident. In the garden of forking paths that is the history of Italian terrorism, we find a few useful ideas. One was the idea of the strategy of tension. The leftists, extremists, and otherwise, theorized in the early seventies, when they were desperately trying to make sense of the weird and frightening succession of events bloodying the streets of Italy, that their right-wing enemy ("rustling in the dark . . . too soon to tell what it is") was trying to destabilize society in a succession of terror attacks, easily blamed on the left, in order to encourage support for a reactionary or even military coup. And look at Italy's neighbors: to the west, Franco's Spain, where the United States had happily encouraged a genuine Fascist regime for a quarter century; to the east, the Greek Colonels, again tacitly supported by U.S. power as a Cold War bulwark against Communism. Responsibility for the deaths of the Years of Lead, in fact, is about equally distributed on the left and right of the political landscape.

It is no accident that with the end of the Cold War, there was a rash of political corruption scandals first in Italy and Japan, then in Germany and France. The United States had made some very questionable bedfellows in its crusade against Communism: in Italy, the Christian Democrats. And back in the years of the Brigand Wars, those same Christian Democrats, and the Italian state in general, had decided that in a landscape of chaotic and nihilistic and retrograde forces, the Mafia and the Church represented two islands of predictable sanity and stability.

Sciascia, the Sicilian author mentioned above, wrote in another editorial, that in reading Borges he had noted the following observation: Borges had always thought that Argentina and Spain had little or nothing in common, but one day two lines he read in *Don Quixote* persuaded him otherwise. The passage from Don Quixote read: " . . . let each answer for his own sins yonder; there is a God in Heaven who will not forget to punish the wicked or reward the good; and it is not fitting that honest men should be the instruments of punishment to others, they being therein no way concerned." Sciascia then wrote that, like Borges, he had always believed that in the "Mafioso way of thinking" (*"sentire mafioso"*) there was nothing particularly Spanish, but these two lines by Cervantes changed his mind as well. The most profoundly Mafioso attitude was that of leaving well enough alone, and everyone minding their own business. One of the profound and lasting ironies in the history of Italian terrorism is that the government, which had founded its own legitimacy on having first triumphed over Fascism (although its own personnel consisted largely of the very same people who had administered that system) and having then opposed Communism, found itself forced to combat terrorism, and then almost as a direct consequence, and with a fairly clear reluctance, to combat the Mafia.

By and large, Italian terrorism is a thing of the past. I say by and large, because the Red Brigades (or the New Red Brigades) struck again in the summer of 2002, killing a professor and economist; it was the second Red Brigade killing in three years (both victims were labor economists; both killings may have made use of the same pistol).

Terrorism ended for any number of reasons, but chief among them was the growing prosperity of the average

Italian. The eighties and nineties were a time of spectacular prosperity in Italy, a time when Italy spawned a variety of new myths with which to market itself: the myth of beautiful Tuscany, the myth of Italian fashion and design, the myth of Italian cooking—all myths based on reality, certainly, but a highly selective slice of Italian reality.

Giorgio's Italy was a different world; it is the Italy I encountered when I first went there in the mid-1970s. The difference extended to every aspect of life.

I remember sitting in a café one summer. I was drinking espresso to the sound of street repairs that filtered in through the open door (the door was covered by the dangling strands of colorful plastic that serve the same function as American screen doors; to enter you push through them the way you used to push through beads in hippie pads); the sounds of street repairs were not unlike the Anvil Chorus. Dressed in blue overalls with folded newspaper hats, workers sat on little wooden benches, where they chipped away at the huge stone cobbles with wooden hammer and steel chisel—a far cry from jackhammers and cement mixers.

Even the social strife that plagued Italy had its charming aspects. In 1976, I lived in Perugia, a central Italian hilltown, where I shared an apartment with a young Italian couple named Michele and Angela. We had also taken in a stray cat, which we fed on angel hair pasta (the cat loved it). Michele was a perfect Italian hippie of the mid-seventies. Skinny, slow-moving, with a recurring heroin problem (the drug was cheap and plentiful, one of the side effects of government tolerance of the Mafia), he wore loose Levi's jeans and black Dr. Scholl's clogs. If this was a landscape straight out of Tolkien, *i fasci* (literally, Fascists) were the dark riders of the Perugian Shire. They wore skintight designer jeans, fitted shirts with huge collars, dark blue ventless blazers, and evil-looking little pointy-toed boots with heels. The crotches of the designer jeans were often sandpapered to make them look bulkier (an intuitive understanding of chiaroscuro seems to come with the territory). They enjoyed beating up Hobbitesque hippies like Michele if they could catch them, and the Dr. Scholl's clogs on the granite cobblestones made Michele ideal prey, easy to hear coming and slow on the getaway.

One day Michele returned home in his socks, clogless. He had been chased by a group of fasci through the streets of central Perugia. His first move had been to leap out of his clogs (noisy and cumbersome they may be, but also very easy to shed) and run; his second had been a stroke of tactical genius. Perugia is a very steep hilltown, and in the streets near the summit, there are buildings seven or eight stories tall that are simply built against the side of the hill. Michele knew of one (his heroin habit may have given him familiarity with easy-to-open street doors and dark staircases) in particular. He darted in the front door, and the fasci stood waiting outside, assuming that he would be forced to come back out onto the street later. What they did not know was that the building had a back door, up on the seventh floor, leading onto the next street uphill.

It was a small world. At least that is what I have to assume from the number of people I met who had had some direct or indirect contact with the world of terrorism. People who had been questioned for the Calabresi killing (at least three); people who had swung *chiavi inglesi*; a woman still holding a torch for her Red Brigades boyfriend who was serving a long prison sentence; General Dalla Chiesa's brother-in-law; close friends of Adriano Sofri. Terrorism seemed very close to home.

In northern Italy, where I lived for a year or so, the father of my girlfriend was a civil engineer. All I knew was that he came home from lunch, regular as a cuckoo clock, this dapper little man in a cardigan, a tie, and a green loden overcoat. He was quiet, mild-mannered, and methodical. He would arrive at 1:30, don felt slippers (the floors were of course marble), and sit down to a hot meal with his family. He would retire from the table at 2:15 to the living room for a little afternoon television and a cup of coffee. He would then wander off for a nap, and on awakening set off at 3:45 to be in the office from 4:00 in the afternoon until 7:30.

All he knew about me was that I was seeing his daughter, and that I was dining frequently with the family. He was courteous but remote. One thing that I noticed about him was that he shredded all his correspondence relentlessly each day. When he arrived for lunch he usually brought the morning mail up from the doorman's desk. After reading it through, he would tear each letter into at least four and sometimes sixteen pieces, only then tossing it into the wastebasket.

At the time I did not know why. But a shadow was cast suddenly and starkly one day when Maria Teresa explained that she and her family were worried about her father because he was working on the design of the new high-security prison of Cuneo, *"il supercarcere di Cuneo,"* which was soon to confine a group of dangerous Red Brigades terrorists. The Red Brigades, who were by no means all in prison, might wish him ill. In fact, various other people who worked on or in the prison did become targets, and I have to wonder if anyone shadowed him the way Giorgio shadowed Engineer Caretto.

Maria Teresa more than once commented bitterly that her father was stupid to keep such regular hours and routines. I could see her point.

I remember very clearly reading the paper the morning of May 13, 1977—the day before the mass demonstration described by Giorgio (where he first fired a gun in the street; the demonstration at which the policeman was shot and killed). In Rome, on the Milvian Bridge, the police had fired into a crowd of demonstrators (the demonstration commemorated, incredibly, the third anniversary of a vote that would allow Italians to obtain divorces; in the years before that, as the film *Divorce, Italian Style* illustrated, murder of a spouse provided the only form of divorce then available) and had killed a nineteen-year-old girl named Giorgiana Masi. I looked at her picture, grainy and black-and-white, on the smudged newsprint, and struggled to understand. I fell in love with almost every nineteen-year-old Italian girl I met. Now the police had killed one in cold blood.

I certainly read about the shootings in Milan described by Giorgio; I also understood the anger.

A particularly striking moment came a few months later, one morning when Angela sat reading the morning paper; I had already seen the front page and knew that it detailed a police shooting in Rome. Four members of N.A.P. (Nuclei Armati Proletari, or Armed Proletarian Cells; the militants of this organization were called *nappisti*) had been sitting eating peaches and reading the newspaper on the steps of a Roman church; a squad of Carabinieri stopped to ask for their papers. The two men fled; one escaped but the other, Antonio Lo Muscio, was killed by machine-gun fire. The two women were beaten savagely, with fists, boots, and the butts of guns; it later emerged that one had been pregnant. After they were taken off to the hospital, there were blood and pieces of flesh on the steps of the church where they had been beaten, according to the newspaper article. It was also reported that the two women had just escaped from a prison outside Naples a few months earlier (prison escapees eating peaches and reading newspapers on the steps of a church, in broad daylight: Italy was a very loose place).

What caught my attention was Angela's reaction: "*Mamma mia, quanto mi dispiace!*" (roughly equivalent to "Oh my heavens, what a shame, what a pity!"). I found the terrorists frightening, but Angela, a young nursing student who wore suede jackets and had impossibly tangled red hair and amazing buck teeth, was dismayed by their capture.

There was one more startling moment with a newspaper that I remember. I was standing in a large square reading the news of the murder of Aldo Moro, the former prime minister who had been kidnapped by the Red Brigades in 1978 and held hostage for fifty-five days until the execution of a death sentence "handed down by a people's court." The popular sympathy for the Red Brigades began to wither sharply after the Moro killing.

It is hard to imagine what Giorgio thinks of things now; or perhaps it is all too easy. When he meets Mario, his friend and comrade from "before," in the trattoria, Mario describes the fantasy of traveling a hundred years into the past or fifty years into the future, but then discards the idea of the future as "pure science fiction." Just twenty years into the future would have revealed a sufficiently improbable scenario: the prime minister of Italy is Silvio Berlusconi, a former cruise-ship crooner and satellite-city developer who had become a television tycoon, broadcasting movies about aircraft carriers traveling in time and sitcoms about perfect families. He is a political ally of the heirs to Benito Mussolini's political tradition.

More "Mysteries of Italy" have emerged (each network news show has its own "Mysteries of Italy" graphics and somber theme music). Convictions were finally handed down in the terrorist bombing in the Bologna train station in August 1980 (the logistical heart of the Italian railroad system at the overcrowded and sweltering high point of the summer holiday rush) that killed close to a hundred, including two American college students. One of the bombers—neo-Nazi terrorists—was named Giusva Fioravanti, a former child star; let's say, for ease of identification, the Richie Cunningham of Italy. The explosives used in the bombing may well have come from a munitions dump connected to the secret NATO-sponsored Gladio stay-behind army.

Just a month earlier, at the end of June, a passenger airliner had vanished into the waters off Sicily, killing eighty-one. It took almost a decade before the wreck was salvaged. The black box voice recorder was still intact; the pilot's last words were, "Look, it's a missi . . . " And here the mysteries pile on, almost like something out of Stephen King: a renegade Libyan jet fighter appears to have been flying over Italian airspace that night, and crashed into the mountains of Calabria; NATO forces were conducting war games that night, with two aircraft carriers in the vicinity, one French, one American; Muammar Qadafi's right-hand man was on a flight from Tripoli to Warsaw that night; radar records were destroyed; several Italian generals stood trial for high treason in connection with the case.

One could go on to delve into the mysteries of the Aldo Moro kidnapping and murder, the details of the P-2 secret Masonic Lodge, or the Neo-Nazi killer who took refuge in Stroessner's Paraguay as an honored guest alongside Mengele, or the astonishing stories of the "deviated" Italian secret services. . . .

To say that the world in which Giorgio made his decisions was a looking-glass world may be excessive, but one detail from the styles and protocols of driving a car in Sicily bears retelling. I visited Palermo in the late 1980s, and noticed that while no one seemed to slow down, much less stop, at red traffic lights, my friend— and other drivers—would stop and look carefully in both directions at green traffic lights. When I asked him why, he looked at me with astonishment. "When I have a green light," he explained patiently, "what do those others have? A red light! And you know they're not going to stop. So I'd better."

And in that world, everything that Giorgio describes makes perfect sense. This is the world in which Giorgio worked; this is the looking-glass system in which his knowledge and analysis propels him into a lurching trolley, his right hand on a gun hidden in his pocket, his left hand gripping a handrail, his eyes focused on the distracted bovine face of a fat police detective whose gross belly bumps against Giorgio at every lurch, as his mind feverishly tries not to follow the logical sequence of the odor of aftershave, taking him back to the bathroom where the detective stood that morning, in his pajamas, methodically shaving to the sound of running water . . . because in a few minutes he and two other terrorists were planning to shoot the detective dead.

I think it is very clear that in this world of darkness, of things rustling just out of sight, of massive power concealing pungent misdeed, we can still find the reasons that Giorgio became a militant, a terrorist, a clandestine.

Antony Shugaar
December 2002

TRANSLATOR'S NOTE

As translator, I have done my best to render the tough, ironic prose that tells Giorgio's story, or as much of Giorgio's story as he is willing to reveal. Giorgio himself says that what he writes here may not be accurate, but he will do his best to make it true. The English may not render every detail of what he wrote—there are tacit and explicit references that are necessarily lost—but I hope it conveys the essence of what he meant.

Because this text arrived without a return address and was published anonymously, and because it claims to be a rare glimpse into a shadowy and secret world, the question naturally arises: is this authentic? There is nothing but internal evidence to corroborate its authenticity, and the devilish variable of avowed unreliability. This narrator, in order to be safe, must be inaccurate.

And yet, on many operative details—the tactic of loaning militants for operations such as the planned shooting of the police detective aboard the trolley, the problems with girlfriends when going underground, the attitude of scorn toward the Red Brigades among members of other terrorist groups—what Giorgio wrote in

1981 was confirmed repeatedly in trial testimony from terrorists in later years.

Some of the discrepancies in the text are probably simple oversight: early on, he refers to the big demonstration where he carried a gun as taking place in March; later he places it in May. In the English, it is placed uniformly in May. In fact, the demonstration took place on 14 May 1977, and would have been immediately recognizable to any reasonably well-informed Italian reader in 1981.

And yet Giorgio clearly sets it in March; later he identifies it as taking place in the correct month. It is as if he were at first being careful, and later relaxing, having decided that the month in which the demonstration occurred was not an important detail.

Similarly, he refers to a distant city, with water instead of streets; in time he openly describes it as Venice; he refers to another city on the coast, filled with marble-lined squares, and then relents, identifying it as Genoa.

He uses the terms trolley and bus interchangably, which may have been common parlance in Milan twenty years ago; but when he says that the 27 trolley makes forty stops, he is right, or close enough to be credible (in the year 2002 it makes thirty-nine stops, but twenty years ago there may well have been a stop or two more).

And finally, he refers to his vacation in the mountains with his family as "once," as if it had happened long ago; by the end of the book you realize that in fact he has written the whole book, or at least a considerable portion of it, in the mountains, in the heart of his family. Each of this instances of initial reticence, followed by disclosure, acts like a camera zooming in, providing detail and intimacy.

Occasionally however they look like oversights, errors in tradecraft.

The single most glaring inconsistency is his supposed fiction of calling his mother and Anna, his ex-girlfriend, on a payphone, pretending to be calling from Rome although he is actually in Milan.

Anyone who used a payphone in those long-ago years to make a long-distance phone call, using the heavy metal Italian phone tokens, would know that the regular clanging sound as the time was used up and the tokens dropped into the coin box is unmistakable. It would be impossible to call someone on a payphone from Milan and pretend to be calling from Rome.

But, again, there may be explanations for this: Giorgio may actually have lived in Rome; he may have been in a third city. It is difficult to say. But this is the only glaring inconsistency that I have been able to find.

The Milan that Giorgio describes is completely truthful and accurate; the left-wing extremist movement is equally plausible.

It would be nice to know if any of the characters in the book recognized themselves: Engineer Caretto, in particular, who had such a close call and would still be around to learn of it. The police detective on the trolley, on the other hand, never learned of his narrow escape, as he had been killed by another cell before Giorgio even wrote his *Memorie dalla Clandestinità*.

Antony Shugaar

PUBLISHER'S NOTE

to the Original Italian Edition, Milan, 1981

A few months ago, in the most recent volume of *Il Pane e le Rose* (Bread and Roses), the editor of the series, Annamaria Caredio, published an appeal, asking the readers to submit their own works of narrative. And so when we received a text with a short and reasonably vague cover letter, signed simply Giorgio, we weren't particularly excited; it seemed like any of the numerous typescripts that had been sent to us in response to our appeal. And in fact, the style of writing and the autobiographical approach were both fairly typical of the literary production of young authors of the Seventies; the story it told was quite another matter, however.

Until now, this kind of story had been described, from the exterior, by sociologists, politicians, and journalists; at most, the shadows were illuminated here and there by the statements of repentant terrorists, but their very renegade status cast doubt on the authenticity of their accounts. Here, for the first time—anonymously, with all the risks of fakery that come with anonymity—we are able to read a complete account from inside the armed struggle.

It was not easy for us to make up our minds whether or not to publish. There was a furious debate within the publishing house, reflecting positions and attitudes toward terrorism that are present on a broader scale throughout Italy today. Although we all unanimously condemn terrorist violence, it became a question of principle. And what finally assuaged our doubts was when we moved from a general debate to a specific judgment of Giorgio's book. We reread it carefully, and the spare, unemphatic prose style, the detailed description of the drab rat race of terror, the anguished loneliness that emerged, stated almost explicitly, brought us back to the concrete terms of the problem. It was not a matter of deciding whether or not to publish a political message from the armed party, but simply whether to publish an account of how a life could be spent that, however chilling, corresponds to a path that hundreds of young people have chosen in recent years. We couldn't turn back.

The Publishers

Dear Comrades,

After reading the note from Annamaria Caredio that was printed at the end of *La Ragazza di Via Millelire,* requesting submissions, I decide to send you this text of mine, which you may perhaps find interesting. It strikes me that, in the surging tide of disinformation, lies, and idiocy that surrounds the world of the armed struggle and its militants, this text may serve at least as a useful document, offering a first-hand account of just how different things are.

I have nothing else to add, except that I hope you publish these pages.

Yours in Communism,
Giorgio

MEMOIRS OF AN
ITALIAN
TERRORIST

In the summer we would go to the beach. (Or maybe we would go to the mountains, or to the country, or into the hills: let me make it clear from the outset, what I write here can't be true, it can only be truthful; and many will understand when I say that telling your own story is a privilege, not an act of courage.)

And so we would go to the beach.

But the beach was always so incredibly far away, and it seems that all I can remember of those distant vacations is an endless dusty road and the merciless heat and the regular noise of my clogs. So many pairs of clogs, so many wet swimsuits, so many beach bags tossed to the ground.

And the smell of doughnuts (or maybe they were fritters or strudels or cakes or foccaccia): the smell of the afternoon comes back to me even today, an afternoon near a pine grove, an afternoon that was too long and too azure, as the poet says.[1]

But a doughnut every day—I wonder, isn't that like no doughnuts at all?

And then there were the crickets (or the cicadas or the blackbirds or the wood grouses).

The crickets would chirp. That's what crickets do, right? They chirp constantly, they never stop. And the children can't sleep, because it's too hot, or at least that's what they say; but they are really just waiting for the crickets. To stop. Chirping.

So this is a vacation. The Red Brigades—people say—give their militants one month's paid vacation. Nobody gives me anything.

This will be my vacation: writing my story, or a story that somehow resembles my story. This too will be an anonymous vacation, one of those vacations you never talk about, just because it's not worth talking about. A vacation that leaves no traces, not even a photograph to remember it by, a photograph with lots of kids covered with black sand, and you can barely recognize yourself, much less any of the others.

What I'd really like to do is go away.

Just leave, take a long long trip somewhere, get away, body and mind, somewhere different. I am so tired, and when you enter this long tunnel that my life has become, you just need to forget the idea of a future. There are no roads out of here.

One way out, of course, would be the Revolution. But let's not kid ourselves. More likely, it will be prison. Or worse. You don't think about it, of course, but then you can hardly imagine going on like this for the rest of your life either. I willingly accept both possibilities: jail, and worse. I don't care in the slightest. In the meanwhile, I take my trip, in my head, and in my books, in the images that I hold on to.

This is the world, reread through my feelings.

My travel companion is Corto Maltese,[2] and there is no point to pretending otherwise. Corto Maltese's China, Corto Maltese's Amazonia—those are the places I want to go.

Corto Maltese's China is a place filled with stone-paved roads, hand-drawn dragons, young girls' slippers. Everywhere you see lanterns and butterflies fluttering over rice paddies. Red lanterns from a time when the Revolution was still possible. From when there were warlords in Russia, from when baronesses traveled through the night aboard trains carrying a sizable share of the Czar's treasure.

It's not the China of posters and mountains leveled for irrigation projects.

And Corto Maltese's Amazonia is a land of the last headhunters and the last of the real adventurers. Corto Maltese's Venice is a city of card-reading fortune-tellers and Freemasons, and Corto Maltese's America—there is no America, it doesn't exist yet. There is only the Orient. Not the mystical Far East, but the Orient of sailing ships, teeming commerce, and true oppressors.

I like a world where something rustles in the dark, where there's something out there, but it's too soon to tell what it is.

A world not unlike the one I actually inhabit now.

You might say everything started with that demonstration in May 1977. I had already been a member for a year and a half of an organization that was in the area of the Autonomia.[3] It was a large and active student organization, and our positions were considerably at variance with the more traditional attitudes of the Autonomia. Nobody referred to it yet as the theory of needs, but for us it was already the way we did things. Our conversations were constantly—you might almost say, obsessively—focused on what we called, and what we still call, behaviors: the lifestyles of young proletarians, the desires that are embedded in those lifestyles, and the forms that they take, like self-expression, the claim to existence, attacks against the system of power. This, this above all other things, was our area of political and cultural interest.

We all or nearly all came from the experience of the Youth Groups,[4] and in those groups we had truly done everything imaginable. From protests to concerts to takeovers to invading movie theaters all the way up to outright theft and psychedelic experimentations, and I am referring to drugs (LSD, especially).

That was where it all started: that was when I left Lotta Continua[5] and I joined the Autonomia. At the time I was very, very much of a spontaneist: I sensed that something very important was developing in the proletarian youth movement, and I believed that any structure was too narrow and too rigid to contain it; that needs and behaviors simply had to "explode." That was the way I thought: *explode*. Without any half measures. This was a phrase that I used, and we all used, all the time. No half measures. While Lotta Continua was always talking about organizing the Youth Groups, I thought that was just intolerable. I thought that if anyone was going to organize the Youth Groups it ought to be the Youth Groups themselves: we should self-organize, in other words.

And that is what we started to do. Here's how. We would all inveigh constantly against the attitude we described as *"miserabilismo,"* against a conception of the labor movement that called for the attainment of bare necessities as it projected an austere, ascetic, rigorous image. And we wanted the opposite; we are all for the excess, we used to say. We wanted everything. We didn't just want bread. At that point, someone would say: "We want roses too." "No," I said during one discussion, "Let us eat cake! Marie Antoinette[6] was right." Everybody liked that a lot. And so we decided to expropriate some blue jeans.

I swear, I wasn't afraid. Not because I am especially brave. That remains to be seen. Because, quite simply, this is how I am: fear might be there before, long before; or else afterward, even a long time afterward; but never during. All things considered, for me fear does not come with thought or even imagination or elaborate fantasizing. And so it might happen that I become terribly afraid six months later, when it happens that my mind touches, by chance, on some detail, an instant, an episode in an action committed or remaining to be committed, or when a dream or a fantasy transmits an image or a face or a gesture.

But if I am busy committing an action, my feelings are entirely focused on the action itself, and there is no time or room for anything else. That's how it was this time, too. I made extremely detailed preparations, though maybe I was the only one who did; for the others, it was as if they were playing a game. Not me. I spent a long time getting ready at home, first of all deciding what I would wear. For two reasons: I wanted to wear the right clothing—so I could move comfortably, easily, fast—and I wanted to satisfy a certain sense of vanity.

It may seem absurd, and ridiculous; maybe it opens me up to irony, speculation, attacks. I can hear them now, saying, "Oh the little gentlemen, getting all gussied up to start a revolution. . . ." But that's how it was. I would never set out to undertake a proletarian expropriation if I didn't feel that I was dressed right, if I didn't feel comfortable: I see nothing odd about that. Dressing well is not what people think: dressing well is feeling comfortable and in harmony with one's clothing, with the cut, the color, and the size. So why shouldn't I try to dress well when I am about to undertake an action, just as I would dress well when I go to the movies? In fact, the very fact that the action is necessarily (and luckily) anonymous proves that choosing one outfit and not another is not a matter of showing off. I remember that on this particular occasion—it was mid-November—I put on a pair of green corduroy trousers—elephant cords—and a heavy ski sweater. And it was weird because everybody else—with the excuse, completely wrongheaded as I saw it, that they shouldn't "stand out"—was wearing clothing that they thought was anonymous and normal, and maybe that clothing was normal, but as soon as they put it on, it seemed strange and outlandish.

Over my sweater, for my part, I wore an enormous red ski windbreaker. And a green ski mask. We made an appointment not far from the boutique, by a phone booth, and that's where we met. I was in charge of the action, even if there was not much leadership involved. There were about a dozen of us, including four girls, all of us very young.

The comrades all gathered at the appointed place separately and at different times. Except that the timing, which was meant as a precaution, nearly turned into a major problem; there were some who showed up—from excessive zeal or simply from carelessness—as much as an hour late, and there we stood, waiting, like a bunch of jerks. All the same, it was incredibly thrilling. There was a feeling in the crowd like the feeling that comes before a huge prank, as well as the sense of complicity that links a group of boys out courting girls their own age. And so we stood there waiting, and one guy would crack a joke, saying, "I'm going to steal a tuxedo"; and another would warn, "Make sure you don't pull out your wallet by mistake on your way out." And a girl would say, "The real problem will be to get colors that match, I certainly don't plan to steal anything I can't wear." And so on.

Finally everyone arrived and I said: "Let's go." And so we walked into the boutique: we milled around a bit so that we were spread out through the two large rooms that made up the store. There were some shoppers, but only a few, and a dozen or so sales clerks, male and female, all young and aggressively stylish. There were two other sales clerks, at the two cash registers. I wandered around for a while and finally came to a stop near a pile of jeans; as long as I was there I figured I would take Levi's. I started looking at the jeans more carefully, as if I were thinking of buying a pair, and the whole time I was saying to myself: "Now. Now. Now."

It was up to me to give the signal. But I hesitated. I kept looking behind me out of the corner of my eye, saying to myself, "A little longer, just another second," and then, "Go!" It occurred to me that my comrades were all looking at me in surprise and concern, and the sales clerks were starting to watch us too. They certainly couldn't guess what we planned to do, but they might have been starting to worry. There might even be an alarm button somewhere in the store. Or a private guard service. Or closed-circuit cameras. And it suddenly dawned on me that if I waited another minute, nothing would happen at all. And so I said to myself: "Now." I straightened up from the pile of pants, just as a clerk, rail-thin, with an especially stupid face, was asking me, "Can I help you? What are you looking for?" In a flash, I pulled my ski mask down over my eyes—we had agreed that would be the signal—and I started shouting, "Send the bill to Andreotti!"[7] All the others started shouting too. I pulled a hammer out of the inside pocket of my windbreaker and said to the clerk, "Don't move, we're liberating this store." The other comrades did more or less the same thing. The girls pulled big trash bags out of their purses and were stuffing into them everything they could grab off the counters. I headed over to the cash registers with another guy, where we cornered the two people who were there, clearly the owners of the store. "We don't want your money," I said, but they kept staring at us in desperation. At the same time, three other comrades stood in front of the door, blocking the entrance to prevent new customers from coming in and cutting off the view from the street, so that what was happening in the store was less visible from outside.

In any case, the whole thing took no more than five minutes. The girls had filled their bags, each one of us had grabbed three stacks of clothing—as much as we could carry in our arms—and I said, "Let's go, everybody move!" The girls were the first to head for the door, then the guys, and last of all, me. Before I went out the door, I set down a plastic bag right next to the door, and in a very loud voice I said, "This is a bomb. Stay close to that wall, over there, and you will be safe." Later, I learned that they really did stay there, hugging the wall. For a full fifteen minutes. As soon as we got outside, we ran off as fast as we could.

Outside, there were a lot of people, you might say a genuine crowd, so we headed off in twelve different directions. Well, maybe not exactly twelve directions, but almost. With my jeans under my arm I ran toward a wide stretch in the road, no more than five hundred meters away. I had left a sports bag there, between two parked cars, covered by a cardboard box. Luckily, the bag was still there. I opened it and I stuffed the jeans into it, and then I walked off calmly carrying the now-heavy duffel bag.

This first action was an important step. For the first time I was committing an illegal act outside of the context of a mass demonstration. And the same thing was true for most of the comrades who took part in it.

Anna was already there. Present, important.

I am a person basically connected to the idea of a family, a stable emotional context. And I have never been reluctant to consider the idea of children. I have never approved—not that I am scandalized, I just don't approve—of what are generally referred to as "open" couples. They strike me as nothing more than messy. Just to offer a bit of cracker-barrel psychoanalysis, it must be true that the family I grew up in left me with a model to aspire to and a sense of regret.

Anna had a way about her that I liked; she was proud and tended to keep to herself. Once you got past her combative manner, her perennial anger, you felt like the sole privileged possessor of something. This was the closest I had ever come to a traditional relationship. Because it aroused in me a desire to win and possess.

I was never bored with that relationship. I never knew on any given occasion, before we would go out together, if that night she was going to be distant with me or affectionate, whether or not we would make love, and if we did, whether she would lie there open-eyed and motionless or whether she'd take part. I really loved her.

She would observe without speaking, or else just say very little. She would look on with a serious, distant expression: "This is all very difficult for me to understand," she would always say. She might say it after hours and hours of listening intently during a meeting, after hours and hours of marching that would make your feet ache. "I really don't understand why." Not that she was cynical. The next time, she would start over: she'd spend hours and hours at meetings, in freezing streets, doing the things that needed to be done—unemotionally, with a relentless mental clarity. I really loved her.

When we rendezvoused later with the others at the

Youth Group, we talked for a long time, and we immediately realized that our action at the boutique marked a
boundary between two different phases of our activity.

First of all, the newspapers: the articles were very clear.
They referred to us as hooligans and criminals, and that
was not a minor point. We were no longer the usual
extremists—political militants, however irresponsible
and violent, but still political militants. Not now; now
we were nothing more than thieves. And we were still
not completely clear what the reaction was among the
other members of the Youth Group and everyone who
had a relationship with the group, the young proletarians of the quarter, especially. We decided to print up a
leaflet. We had to choose whether to make it a leaflet
issued by the Youth Group itself, in which case we could
only speak in very general terms about the action
without claiming responsibility (to do any differently
would mean admitting our guilt for a criminal act and
exposing ourselves to repression), or whether to claim
responsibility for the action anonymously.

We opted for the latter course. We immediately were
faced with the logistical problem of the mimeograph
machine. We couldn't very well mimeograph a leaflet
and then leave the mimeograph machine lying around
for the police to find, since they could easily match it to
the leaflet. And so, since we could not get our hands on
another mimeograph machine, we decided to use the
Youth Group's machine and then hide it somewhere. I
was the one who suggested hiding it, and then I added,
in pretty clear terms, that doing something of this sort
meant, in a certain sense, "going underground." That is,

it meant creating a structure outside the law. At the time, nobody worried about it. We decided that we were going to hide the mimeograph machine in a storage carrel in the basement where one of the group lived. And so we prepared the leaflet. It was very nice and it was very well received in the neighborhood, among the kids, of course; we had even included some drawings, and the style, all things considered, was quite ironic. The result was that many of the young people in the neighborhood came to us and asked us if they could buy clothing at a discount. We would go ahead, with a few precautions, and give them the clothing outright. The unbelievable thing is that, as careful as we had been, we came very close to getting caught. The way it happened was this: The mimeograph machine was supposed to be hidden immediately, but then something unexpected came up (the way something unexpected always comes up)—they couldn't find the key to the storage carrel, or something like that—and so, two days after we distributed the leaflets, the mimeograph machine was still sitting there in the Youth Group office. On the third day—to be exact, on the third night—we moved it to the basement, and the police came to search the very next morning, exactly six hours after the machine had been moved. And so I gave a lot of thought to how the whole thing had gone; I carefully considered the entire action, the secondary details, the mistakes we had made, and the things we had done right. And I scrupulously went back over all of my actions; I even took notes and talked things over with those I considered my most trusted and determined comrades. And I believe that this was when I decided that I would no longer hesitate or hold back. During this action, I had carried an air pistol, a Flobert. I carried it in my jacket pocket just in case something totally unexpected occurred—an unexpected reaction, a private guard, anyone who tried to stop us. The Flobert is not even a real pistol, you might say; or perhaps it is a real pistol, but one for kids and ladies. It can't kill or even injure anyone seriously, and in fact you don't even need a license to buy one. You go to a gun store, you buy it, you give your name, and that is the end of it. You could even give a fake name, since nobody bothers to check.

Piero and I took that Flobert to the beach two or three times. We practiced shooting until we could use it perfectly, hitting any target, even at a run, and at short range, because farther away than twenty meters the Flobert tends to be very inaccurate. Then we bought another gun, again an air pistol, and so it happened that we went armed to a number of demonstrations. Armed, in a manner of speaking, but armed all the same. It seemed like a major step to us. We moved together, from the first minute to the last, with our pistols in the pockets of our jackets and our hands on the handles, but for one reason or another we never had a chance to use them. And it may be that deep down we were relieved. Then we decided to "raise our fire."

Those were the words we used: "raise our fire." And we used them quite seriously, because to us this meant moving forward, continuing the process, radicalizing. It meant, in fact, *raising our fire.* It meant carrying real pistols. And we did it very soon thereafter.

Forget about *come forward for a moment, you unknown*

ones, with your faces masked. This is unquestionably something for other times and other men.

Not that there is no longer a need for masked faces
(otherwise, why would I be among them?)
it's just that to say it like that is laughable and sad,
like something old
or the Festa dell'Unità at the Bovisa.
Or it hurts the heart, the hands, and the genitals.

Because heart, hands, and genitals ache,
ache so much, if you constantly deny them and hide
    them
like absurd vices you are trying to forget:
because there has been time enough and there will
    always be time enough to
cover them, and you would finally like
to let them breathe freely in the open air.

That is what I want, I who—you might say—barely
    found time
to pass from covering my face
to hide the pimples and acne,
and covering my hands
to conceal awkwardness and fear,
and covering my genitals to hide blushing and
    reluctance:
to now, when I cover body and face to conceal the
    fact that . . .

The blue jeans proved useful. We had hidden a fair

number in Piero's house, not knowing ourselves what we would do with them; there were also sweaters, shirts, and shoes.

We wrapped them up in two large packages and went to the Fiera di Senigallia. We sold both packages at the first booth we stopped at for a hundred thousand lire. And we decided that we would buy ourselves a real handgun. But a hundred thousand lire was just not enough money.

I carried out the second important action. Piero was, is, from a wealthy family; not incredibly rich, but definitely well-to-do. We decided that the easiest thing to do was to break into a drawer in the dresser in his parents' room where they kept their cash.

And that's what we did. One Sunday morning, Piero was supposed to drive with his family to Camogli, where they own a house. When they were already in the car and were about to leave, he said that he had forgotten a textbook in the apartment. He ran upstairs, grabbed the book, and left the apartment door open behind him. He did this for two reasons: first of all, when we found out that the whole family would be going to Camogli, it was already Saturday afternoon, so it was no longer possible to make a copy of the key; and second, we didn't want to use Piero's key because of possible complications. Indeed, sometime that Sunday, Piero would find a way of letting it be noticed that he still had his key. And so, an hour after the family left, I was standing outside the apartment house, and when the main street door opened to let in an old lady who was clearly coming home from Mass, I slipped in after her. I climbed slowly to the fourth floor, and as we had agreed, I found the door ajar. I wandered through the apartment, finally coming to a halt in the bedroom of Piero's parents. In their dresser, there was just one drawer with a lock. I had taken a large screwdriver from a cabinet near the kitchen, and it was really easy to pry the drawer open with it. All I had to do was shove the tip of it in on a line with the lock and push. The drawer popped open after a couple of seconds of pressure.

I remember an odd feeling when I opened the drawer. It was clearly where Piero's mother kept her things, and inside there were vials of feminine perfumes, and the aroma wafted through the room as if they had been miraculously liberated by my hands. Like a magic treasure chest, I thought, or Aladdin's lamp.

Under a stack of white handkerchiefs, also carefully perfumed, there was a large billfold; I opened it and found five banknotes of one hundred thousand lire each. Then one of those strange things that happen to me every so often occurred. I didn't bother to straighten everything up, I didn't hurry out of there, I didn't check to make sure I had left no evidence. Quite simply and greedily, I started rummaging through the drawer. I found packets of letters wrapped up with a rubber band, photographs from various periods and places, official identity documents. I began to paw through the letters, as if I had fallen prey to a morbid curiosity. Let me say it again: this is something that happens to me frequently, perhaps while I am working, when I am shadowing someone or checking out a location. Or even during the course of an action. What happens is that, quite undramatically, I become distracted—but in an all-exclusive, totally absorbing way. All my energy and nerves, which until then had been completely focused on a man or a place or an action to be performed, will suddenly shift *elsewhere*, and they are devoted to that *elsewhere* without reservation. And that *elsewhere* might be a woman, or a shop window, or, when I am in a certain mood, even a monument, an architectural detail, the façade of a church. But to come back to the letters: they all started with the words "Cara Sandra," and they were clearly addressed to Piero's mother, and they were love letters. I immediately realized that they were not all in the same handwriting, and weirdly, I found it amusing, as if it were obscene to discover that Signora Sandra, Piero's mother, had had a number of boyfriends. Then I saw other envelopes with names on them: *To Piero*, *To Letizia*, and then the names of Piero's other brothers and sisters. I went ahead and opened those letters, too. They were little testaments, messages for a later day. The letter to Piero was the most ridiculous; it was full of phrases like "you, the most rebellious of my children," "you, who remind me of my poor brother." At first, I was amused to read them; then I started to feel ashamed. It started to seem indecent to rifle that way through scents, letters, papers, and photographs. But then I decided that it was a useful way to create confusion, and I decided to really turn the drawer inside out. I took all the letters out of their envelopes; I yanked the tops off of all the dozens of boxes—of every shape and size and color imaginable— that were in the drawer; I opened all the other drawers as well. Then I ran from room to room, throwing everything into disarray to make it look like someone had been searching feverishly, creating a haphazard and superficial disorder in the bookshelves, closets, and hutches. Finally, with the screwdriver, I gouged the entry door around the keyhole to simulate an imaginary break-in, and then I left, after carefully pulling the door shut so that the damage would not be noticed any sooner than necessary. That is when the second absurd thing happened: for whatever reason, I took the elevator. Absurd because I hadn't taken the elevator to go up, and absurd because I had refrained from taking it intentionally—who knows?—in order to keep from being seen.

And so, while I was riding the elevator down, suddenly everything went dark and I felt the elevator come to a halt. Oh God, I thought, just like in *Elevator to the Gallows*.[8] I sat there in the dark for a few minutes, trying to think where I could hide the five hundred-thousand-lire bills, if I needed to. I carefully felt the ceiling of the elevator cab and realized that there was a hollow space that would make a perfect hiding place. I decided that I would use it if I had a chance and if it became necessary. After a few more minutes, the elevator was still motionless. It was still completely dark, and I felt a vague sense of foreboding. So I decided to feel all the various buttons; I assumed that the alarm button must be the last one. I thought to myself that if I was questioned, I would say that I was a friend of Piero's and that I had found the main door of the apartment building open and that I had gone up to his apartment but that nobody was home. I pressed the alarm button. There was a long ringing sound. After a short interval I heard a voice yelling, "What floor are you on?" A few minutes later, I heard the sound of keys and someone opened the door. Then I had to pull myself up to the second-floor landing, helped by a heavyset fellow in an undershirt—unquestionably the porter. He was so annoyed at being disturbed during his one day off that he didn't even ask me who I was. And so I left without any further ado.

Now we had six hundred thousand lire. We thought that with that much money we could buy two handguns at the Fiera di Senigallia. Actually, that is not how things happened.

At the Fiera di Senigallia they took us for idiots or possibly for plainclothes police officers, and they tried to sell us either old rusty pistols or else toy pistols: real toy pistols, meaning toy pistols for children. But through an Autonomo, with whom we had had meetings when we were trying to organize the Youth Groups, we managed to get our hands on two handguns. Two small revolvers. And the same Autonomo—a guy who politically was close to the anarchists, a Comontista,[9] or something of the sort—offered to let us use them.

We went with him on two separate occasions, on the road toward Pavia, along the Navigli: it wasn't hard at all.

That was the first time that we went armed to a demonstration. The demonstration was a demonstration unlike any other, different from the harshest demonstrations of the Autonomia. We realized this when it dawned on us that there were a great many of us carrying guns. In reality, we didn't know exactly what to do. We knew that if the police fired, we would shoot back. We had decided that we would do this, and we were determined to follow through.

That was all, but it was a lot. The slogans we chanted were particularly violent and radical. And so, when we got close to San Vittore, I understood that something had to happen, that something was going to happen, and, to tell the truth, it wasn't really very difficult to figure it out. We had decided, without needing to talk about it or plan anything out in particular, that we were not going to give way to any show of force; and it was pretty clear that there were going to be shows of force. The prohibition against marching to the prison of San Vittore, for instance, was pretty obvious. And so when we saw the cordon of policemen blocking our path, I looked at Piero and it was as if we said to each other: "Done." But we still didn't dare to draw our guns.

In a way, we never specifically dared to draw our guns. In the sense that I cannot remember even now— and yet I continue, but every so often, only once in a while, to think about it—when the "moment" came. It was an awareness more than a decision. I realized that there were others who, like me, were carrying guns. Like me because, in fact, I had drawn my gun. I didn't even have time to look at Piero. I know for certain, even then I knew for certain, that he was doing the same things that I was doing. And that he felt the same way I felt. The action boiled down to an instant: a leap to the middle of the pavement, a tiny pause, shoot, go. That was it. I noticed that up ahead someone, like me, was moving fast. I was already running, with Piero beside me.

Via Carducci is long and wide, and while we were running, fleeing, it was even wider and emptier, already practically dark. I wasn't even slightly afraid; I was running easily, with no effort. There was something behind me that I was running away from, but it wasn't fear. My only thought was to reach the rest of the demonstration. But while I was running, one step after the other, my throat tightened with a secret, private feeling: I felt like laughing, smiling, jumping into the air.

"Piero, Piero, wait for me," I started to call out, to keep from laughing. I was almost ashamed of the kind of contentment that was spreading inside me. Hell, it was nothing, absolutely nothing, just something that resembled happiness—breathing deeply, my chest full of clean air.

Anna was studying medicine, by her own choice and with enormous determination. The evening of the demonstration I was still stunned and happy, and I called her up.

"When can I see you?"

"Right now, come by my house," she answered immediately.

She knew my political positions, and she held many of the same views. And yet that evening we had a ridiculous clash, extremely annoying.

We went to drink an aperitif in the most luxurious bar in Milan. The waiter brought us cocktail sandwiches, pickled onions, potato chips, and olives. Anna was very nicely dressed, and she prattled on: I was squirming in my seat from sheer boredom. She was doing it on purpose, I believe.

"Little ladies from good Milanese families always wear

light blue," I cut her short. "But you forgot to put on your collar."

"The collar is something quite different, I think. My shoes don't match, for that matter. I don't have any dark-blue shoes. I don't approve of what happened today. Were you there?"

"How about you?"

"Of course I was."

"So why do you ask me if I was there?"

"Because I didn't see you, and I was looking for you."

"You were with the wrong people." I could no longer conceal my irritation with this young aspiring doctor.

"Maybe you were with the wrong people. Somebody was killed."

"A policeman."

"Someone. Or maybe I should say, a person. These things disgust me and they frighten me. Where were you? I didn't see you, or Gianni, or Piero either. You must have gone with the crowd that split off, otherwise I would have seen you afterward. But I don't know what you did. What did you do?"

"Do you want to have a debate on proletarian violence? Do you want to know what the newspapers will write tomorrow?"

"Don't start again with the newspapers—"

"Do you want me to tell you whether I agree or disagree with the shooting? Exactly what does your middle-class sense of propriety want to know?" My voice kept rising and then dropping. Every once in a while it would break from the tension that I was feeling. But I could never accept the tone that she was using. This was exactly what I most hated about her: when that remoteness of hers was nothing more than the middle-class superiority of someone who has always lived in the expensive heart of the city.

"And even if I did something, anything, what do you care? Do you mean to tell me that you have ever bothered to try to understand, not just judge?"

"If you don't lower your voice everyone will turn and stare," she interrupted, "and if you really were with the group that split off today, I would recommend that you start considering other people as potential witnesses. If you really plan to move in that direction, my advice is to start being a little more careful. Or are you just doing it, like you always do, to be able to tell yourself that you are doing it? If that's your reason, let me give you one last piece of advice: start hanging out in the bars in your own neighborhood. They found out a long time ago that it's possible to boast about things without necessarily doing them." She got up. "At any rate, this whole story leaves me completely cold. I am not interested in listening to you drone on with your ideological sermons. I have had enough of that from everyone I've been with in the past few years. And if you aren't interested in talking, then there's no point in going on. In a few years, maybe you can come talk to me for a fee."

And with a style that was uniquely hers, she got up, put two thousand lire on the table, and left, her light-blue outfit making her a girl from a respectable family.

News of the death of the policeman spread quickly. We did not hold a meeting. Not because there was a decision not to. On the contrary. We all acted like we were entirely certain of our actions. The police had provoked us. The prohibition was intolerable.

The government in Rome was holding an entire nation in a state of siege. And then we were really much more pissed off with those assholes from the MLS[10] who had beaten with monkey wrenches everyone suspected of having split off from the main group. Confident judgments, in short, flowed like water. But deep down there was a slight fear of meeting in one place. I don't know if that fear was only because of the risk of police searches or raids. Now I tend to think there was another kind of fear—the fear of being forced to talk things over, for example. That is an idea that I venture to suggest only now. At the time, in reality, I was just very tired. I only wanted to talk to Piero.

"Where'd you put it?"

"I didn't hide it. Why? Should I have?"

"No, not really."

"Were you scared?"

"No, at least I don't think so."

The grass was wet and pulpy underfoot, the way it is in May, in the evening, in Milan. Piero was almost embarrassed. Almost as much as I was.

"You all right?"

"Never been better." Piero kept answering angrily. "Never been better. In fact, I'm worried about how fine I feel." He turned away.

"This time we did it. But I don't regret it even a bit. What about you?"

Ah, the way that city belonged to me in that instant, in

that park, with that friend close to me—it's never been that way since. Not even afterward, when I had learned every corner of the city, in my endless days of shadowing and studying the obscure daily routes of so many obscure individuals.

The history of those first pistol shots actually began the next day. Naturally, it was on the front page. And the local Milanese section of the *Corriere della Sera* ran a headline that read: "The Autonomi used sawed-off shotguns to attack the police." There was a photograph of a building on fire. A photograph of part of the demonstration. Autonomi? That was not the first time that the word had been used as a synonym for criminals and troublemakers. But this time it was also being used to mean "terrorists." I had never considered the events of those months from that point of view. From my point of view, the things that happened to me had other names. For me, they were the names of the local Youth Group, who bore the sort of anger and disappointment that had been widespread in the official political groups, and the names of my friends. Everything had other names and other times for me. Time, especially, was different. I hadn't sensed any shift in myself, the Youth Group, the jeans store, the purchase of the gun, and the demonstration of the day before. But something must have happened yesterday, if I was on the front page being called a terrorist.

The *Corriere della Sera* was still open, in my hands, right in front of the newsstand. A newsstand that was a long way from my usual newsstand. Without even realizing it,

I had begun to put into practice what I would later consider one of the basic daily rules of underground security. I was holding the *Corriere della Sera*, which angrily
described an episode that, to me, yesterday, had been
thoughts, the sensation of running, a half-smile that had
come to my lips against my will. I felt as if I was split in
two: me on paper and me yesterday. I folded up the
paper and ran back over the previous day in my mind,
street by street, corner by corner.

The prohibition against marching to San Vittore was
clear. Democrazia Proletaria[11] and the others had
established in advance that it would be a "peaceful
mass demonstration," as the phrase went in those days.
The formula was a message to the authorities, but especially to us. And we, of course, had ignored the
warning, this time and other times previously. It was a
strange way of being part of the movement, typical of
all the surviving groups; a weird form of cannibalism,
it seemed. Everybody—big bosses and little bosses—
had done their best to try to direct something where
you were in but you were also out. Because in the final
analysis, the problem was whether you acted or didn't,
not whether someone could decide what someone else
would do. But they had failed to understand that. And
so, with a certain embarassment, doing their best to
conceal the way in which they were no different from
what they always had been, they kept criticizing us.
There were no longer any official group meetings, but
the air was still full of agreements, priorities, little and
big senior leaders.

And we didn't care in the slightest.

We who? I can't say. The "Autonomi," as far as I was concerned, meant me and the people I knew. There were others. I imagine all of them were just like me, there, more or less, without any preliminary agreement about being there. The others had showed up, but I always worked side by side with Piero. And this, I later learned, is another fundamental rule of the armed struggle: you must operate with someone else in perfect concert, as if with another self. The *Corriere della Sera* that morning said that there were three hundred of us. In reality, we were far more numerous than that. The question of numbers is an old habit of the old political groups; they were always counting others and counting themselves. I couldn't care less. And yet, every so often, automatically, I find myself caring about the numbers, because deep down I am proud. So yesterday, we were right here. We lined up, amid a general feeling of dislike. I held back even further. Even among us a number of gurus had sprung up, venerable chiefs of the official Autonomia, who would walk up ahead, maintaining a link between the two sections of the demonstration.

Oreste would run up ahead and then come on back. He is always active, extremely active, almost annoyingly active. He never stands still, and he is constantly offering organizational suggestions. My pistol was weighing heavily in my pocket. My first real gun in a demonstration. Here, in Via Carducci, we split off. Corso di Porta Vercellina. Viale Papiniano. Piazza Sant'Agostino. I didn't look at the names of the streets yesterday. I was waiting from one moment to the next for an obstacle, a snag. How would I react? Via Olona.

I read in the paper that the conductor of the 97 trolley is named Lino Baracchi, age thirty-seven. That asshole, I don't know what he thought he was trying to do yesterday. But for that matter, I don't know what the others thought they were trying to do. The 97 came to a stop practically right in front of us. A group surged forward and blocked it. I followed the surge. I climbed on and there was no reason to push; all of the passengers had retreated. I went to talk to this Lino Baracchi, accompanied by two other comrades. A little bit after that, a few bottles shattered in front of the trolley. After they burst into flame, it was just a second before we saw motion at the far end of the street. Oreste had planted himself a little further along, ahead of us, arms spread wide, yelling, "Let's stay with the demonstration, comrades, let's stay." What did he want? This is where we were supposed to be. The police were forming a dark mass at the end of the street. I heard shots and more shots. I heard my own gun going off. Motionless, in the middle of the street, I fired.

A photograph from that day was published, causing considerable uproar: two Autonomi firing in the middle of an empty street. One is bent forward, bracing his arm as he takes aim; the other has already turned to run, twisting his head back to look as he does. That's what I must have looked like. That's what Piero looked like; white pants, a sweater. Once again, that image of me, stolen from me and projected outward. Frozen in an act that I performed and that, somehow, I don't recognize in this photograph. That act for me was natural, obvious, and in a sense it had been decided within me long, long before. Now I see that same act caught, captured, and blocked forever—gigantic, even though it was an infinitesimal act. And large and motionless, it is given another name: "terrorism."

Well, between me and them, a definitive line has been drawn.

My entry into the organization was extremely easy. It is funny to consider how much fantasizing and mystification is spun about the matter now—all the inventions and exaggerations that are used to portray an act that is, in fact, as simple as can be. Almost disappointingly ordinary. The popular imagination is probably stimulated once again by ignorance and naïveté. Ignorance about just what Milan was like three, four, five years ago. Well, it is no exaggeration to say that in Milan in those days there were lots and lots of folks who would go to their local trattoria every evening carrying handguns; or who, after going to eat in their local trattoria, would decide to go get a handgun. In the sense that they would go to steal a handgun. It was incredibly easy to do that. Almost ridiculously easy. Among us, the saying was, "You should get guns where you find them." And someone, a bit more of a jokester, would say, borrowing a phrase that was used commonly in the press and mouthed by politicians, "There are too many guns on the street . . . luckily."

And so we would go and get the guns in question. The time we chose was usually the time that is traditionally considered proper; that is, four in the morning—too late for nightowls, too early for the early birds. The customary target was one of two: the railway police or private security guards.

One evening we went to Pavia and ate in a magnificent trattoria in the Oltrepò (I remember it like it was yesterday; we ate snails and drank an amazing quantity of wine). On the way back, we pulled over in a country road, and it was so hot that we decided to go look for someplace where we could cool off. We lay down in a grassy field and five minutes later we were sleeping like babies. I woke up and realized it was two-thirty in the morning; I was starting to feel a little chilly. I woke up the two others and we decided to head back to town. Fifteen minutes later we were in Milan.

Piero, who was driving, evidently didn't feel like going to bed, however, and we kept driving around the city aimlessly. We wound up on the outskirts of town again. The streets were completely deserted; even the watermelon stands were closed, and on the sidewalks there was nobody, nobody at all. I was the one who spotted him. He was a private security guard and he was oddly different from his usual colleagues; this one was kind of old. Maybe he wasn't fifty yet, but he was certainly older than forty. He was walking slowly down one of those pretentious streets that they now have on the outskirts too, where all the "richest" shops are lined up, one alongside the other: the jewelery store, the fur shop, all the way down to the fine delicatessen with caviar in the display window.

He would stop in front of the rolled-down metal grates, and in each one he would slip the night watchman's ticket. At his side there dangled a handsome white holster that gleamed against his dark uniform and looked enormous. And I said: "Disarming him would be like stealing ice cream from a child." That's what I said, without thinking about it too carefully and without planning to suggest anything. Andrea replied: "Okay." Andrea was at least three years older than me and was certainly more experienced than we were; not only was he more experienced than us, he was probably more experienced than anyone I knew. More than once I had thought that Andrea, most likely, was involved in some underground organization; his unwillingness to discuss a certain part of his life confirmed my belief and made me respect him even more. We had driven about half a kilometer when we decided to do it.

We made a wide turn, we drove back on the next street over, we parked the car. We decided that it was a good idea for someone to remain at the wheel, and we agreed that Piero would stay behind. Andrea and I walked toward the street where we had seen the security guard. The plan was pretty simple. Andrea hid in a half-closed street door close to the intersection with another street, and I waited around the corner. I was not supposed to let the guard see me until he reached the end of the block, to maximize the element of surprise.

It all went smoothly—smooth as silk. Without a hitch. I waited around the corner and listened as his footsteps drew closer. When I judged that he was about two meters away—and therefore a meter past the street door where Andrea was hiding—I stepped around the corner and walked toward him. I said the first foolish thing that came to mind: "Do you know where Corso Garibaldi is?" (I knew it was many miles from there.) I asked in a very relaxed and friendly tone of voice. He was startled by the sudden sound and my unexpected appearance, but not so badly startled that he was alarmed or started to reach for his gun. He didn't seem to be a very fast-moving or fast-thinking character, and in any case the holster was fastened shut. I saw Andrea behind him: he was holding a monkey wrench, which he stuck into the guard's back. "Hands up, or I'll shoot," he said, and the guard obeyed immediately. I walked over to him, reached out, unfastened the flap of the holster, and grabbed the big revolver. Andrea said to him, "Inside," and pushed him toward the street door where he had been hiding. The whole thing was done without the guard getting a look at Andrea's face or his imaginary gun. Once he was inside the street door, we tied him up, so to speak; we tied his wrists together with a bandanna and jammed another bandanna into his mouth. In reality, all we needed was for him to keep still for thirty seconds. We told him to sit on the ground. When we emerged from the street door and turned the corner, there was Piero with the car. We jumped in and two minutes later we were far away, in a fever of excitement and glee. At least Piero and I were. Andrea seemed calmer, and maybe even a little worried. But he denied it when I asked him. The revolver was big and shiny, and I did not feel like going to sleep. But Andrea insisted. "You can't drive around the city with a freshly stolen pistol," he said. We all went to sleep.

The next day Andrea came to see me. We went toward the Ticinese neighborhood and then along the Naviglio Grande. This was the first time that Andrea had come to see me; I was still bubbling with excitement, and I said to him right away, "Well then? What do we do next?" He answered abruptly, "This is not a game." I understood that he wasn't kidding. He started to talk, and he asked me to listen carefully.

He described in minute detail everything we had done the night before. He listed all the mistakes we had made (the fuckups, he called them) and the incredible good luck we had had; these aren't things you do on the spur of the moment, and you definitely don't do them in a car with real license plates. It was our good fortune, he said, that the security guard was working alone, since they usually work in pairs and they usually have a car and drive even short distances; that security guards are usually young and strong, as well as courageous, sometimes even reckless; that pretending a monkey wrench is a gun usually doesn't work. I didn't really understand. Or really, I was slowly beginning to understand and I was already guessing where all this was leading. And my guess was correct. Andrea asked me if I was ready to start doing things in a more serious fashion. And he said— and I quote his exact words, "Do you want to enter our organization?" And he added quickly, "Don't answer right away; think about it for three days, then you can tell me." And he refused to answer my questions.

Not even the basic question that I asked immediately: "Which organization are you talking about?"

I continued to assume that he was talking about the Red Brigades and I had very profound misgivings. And so, after three days had passed, our conversation was quite different from what I expected. I told him that I was ready to do things on a serious basis, to make some radical decisions, but that their way of thinking left me cold.

"Our way of thinking?" said Andrea. "Ours, whose?" When I said, "You know, the Red Brigades'," Andrea burst out laughing (and he didn't laugh much; he usually seemed almost sad). He explained things carefully, and three days later I was a member.

In general, there are two ways of dealing with your woman when you go underground: either you both go underground together or you break up. With someone like Anna, the first option was unthinkable. She was immune to all forms of enthusiasm, and she would not have followed me in any undertaking that demanded an element of blind trust, if not faith. There was also a trace of the traditional thought process that men usually follow in this sort of matter: I was looking upon my involvement as the kind of thing women shouldn't take part in. Instead, it revolved around a relationship of male comraderie, a matter of secret complicity that you can only share with other men. With her, in any case, I would need to present a certain façade, so as to place a layer of protection, or intermediation, between her and the truth. This meant, however, that I couldn't show that I was afraid, or upset, or even that I could confide any doubts. And that was not the state of mind I was in. Anyway, I don't really know what it was. In the end, maybe, it may have come down to what I said first: she was too wide awake and clear-eyed, while I—much more than she—was living in a constant yearning for something. I was, in short, if not more fanatical, then at least more unrequited than she was.

The transition to living underground, then, was also a progressive crisis for the two of us. Every couple has this sort of crisis. And we were like any couple. For a while we didn't talk. And in part it was because my new "work" demanded a lot of time. Let's be clear, for a long time nothing remarkable happened. Aside from Andrea, I met only one other militant, my immediate "superior" in the sector to which I had been assigned. I went on living at home, though I was shown an apartment where I was supposed to keep my papers and documents. This was not a terrorist "den" (to use the charming term that reflects, ridiculously, the "typical" culture of the bourgeois journalist and places us somewhere between the secret society and cat burglars); it was just a normal apartment of a normal comrade, who was not a member of the organization and possibly not even aware that I was.

But the "work" itself was grueling. I had been assigned, and it had not been my choice, to the "manufacturing sector" (let's call it that), and at first I was supposed to do nothing more than to study *in depth* a given industrial sector—or rather, as I was instructed, to analyze carefully "the class makeup and capital makeup" of that sector. Which meant, in concrete terms, reading and understanding an endless quantity (at least it seemed endless to me) of books, magazines, and newspapers. Taking notes, making footnotes, summarizing, rephrasing, and boiling it all down. And I did my work, for the most part, with a diligence that bordered on the obsessive, proportionate to my previous almost overwhelming lack of interest—and therefore ignorance—for all that *culture*. And though at the beginning, of course, my stubborn determination was in part due to the obvious psychological elements—my desire to make a good impression, to win the respect and confidence of this still largely unknown organization—little by little I also gained a genuine respect (though never love, never enthusiasm) for this *culture*, the importance and meaning of which I was discovering to be incomparably greater than everything I had previously thought of as culture.

Not that there weren't moments of total discouragement, let me be clear. One, which came on a daily basis, came from reading the newspaper. I had become in some sense accustomed to the idea that books and magazines were boring, or at least potentially boring, but I had a genuine love affair with newspapers. For me reading the newspaper had been, until then, one of the unquestionably pleasurable moments of my day. And now, that moment was being reduced, rapidly and almost exclusively, for want of time, to reading (and certainly not the rapid and often distracted kind of reading that we often devote to a newspaper) the business, financial, and labor pages (the pages that I had almost always skipped in the past) of several major daily papers; and especially the intense study of the pages of *Il Sole/24 Ore.*[12]

I later discovered that reading *Il Sole/24 Ore* was not an isolated obsession of my section or of my organization, but instead a collective fixation of our "circle"; and after a while I clearly understood how significant and appropriate it was.

But in the early days, I'll admit it, when—after I had shaved and had my coffee—I would open the paper, well, I felt like crying.

Anyway, if I have succeeded, at least in part, in giving some idea of how I lived in that first period underground, then it will be clear that many of the questions that people might want to ask me don't make a lot of sense.

What did you feel? What were you thinking? Why did you "cross over"?

That is the point, there wasn't any "crossing over," except that I stopped reading *Lotta Continua*[13] and I started reading *Il Sole/24 Ore* instead. Or that I never had much time for my friends or for girls, but if I had enrolled in medical school, it would have been the same.

At the same time, the "routine" and "boring" activities of that period definitely prepared me for other activities, the ones that people think of when they talk about "crossing over." And not through some subtle mechanism of attraction, progressively sucking you in and involving you in something you can no longer escape, but because only in this way (and I understood this later, obviously) could I understand whether hatred, anger, and rebellion were the product first and foremost of *reason*, if they possessed a core of reason that could guide and consolidate them.

All the way to killing or kneecapping someone, definitely, but as decisions dictated by reason and humanity.

Yes, said in utter seriousness, *the meaning of the death of an oppressor is written in the pages of* Il Sole/24 Ore.

• • •

It was Anna who finally called me back. In that period, I began to alternate evenings at home with evenings out. Home was useful to me; it was still a situation of tranquillity, as well as "normality." They never pried at home. I would drop a hint now and then, so that they would think I was out with Anna, whom my folks knew. I was out when she called, and I didn't bother calling her back. And so, when she finally reached me, more time had passed, more suspicion had sprung up, new distances had developed between her and me. She asked me to come to her house, because her parents had gone to the seaside for the weekend.

That Saturday and Sunday, stolen from her parents, will stay with me always. She seemed to be reassured by the familiar furniture and rooms, and her personality untensed a bit. She took on a gentle and hospitable manner, but behind her way of welcoming me there was also still a reference to a possible life together that was impossible to put into words, except in allusive, ironic terms.

I have always loved Saturdays. Something relaxes inside me on Saturday. On Saturday, it is right not to work. On Saturday, it is right to be lazy. If you feel guilty about being empty-headed during the week, on Saturday it is actually obligatory. The air becomes a little clearer. There is less noise, and so a few things become human again. You can fool yourself that there is no longer a need to scramble day after day. At such a slow pace, in such a beautiful city, in these wonderfully empty streets, you could even find the time to study, or to find an apartment with a garden. In the center of town, even, so you don't waste time taking long trolley rides. Indeed, why not? What need is there to live in a shithole day in and day out? It could be Saturday every day of the week, if I only decided to leave, to abandon everything and do like Michele, who lives in the country.

In the country, but without the nonsense of a new ideology. In the country, because I want to live the way people have always lived, with time to do things, with life and death as part of a natural cycle, to live like one human being among many.

But in my thoughts every delightful sunny Saturday morning, there were always the reflected thoughts—however distant and remote—of the other days of the week. In the countryside, like a couple of assholes. Like the people who turn into journalists, intellectuals, travelers. In the countryside, doing what? And where? Where is this countryside where living and dying are still part of a natural cycle of life?

When Anna opened the door to me that Saturday, the effort of these thoughts had already become too much—too much after a week spent in a sort of sensory deprivation, made up of an artificial capacity to feel everything to excess.

Anna alone was made of flesh and blood, there in front of me, she alone. She opened the door; I wrapped my arms around her, I closed the door while we were still locked in an embrace, and I lowered her slowly beneath me to the hardwood floor. Without undressing myself or her, I sought out the warmth of her legs, her belly, her breasts, rummaging and squeezing, without even feeling the need to make love. And, respectable girl from a respectable family though she may have been, she didn't lift a hand to stop me.

That was Anna, who always understood everything.

Anna was not all I was losing to this new life.

The entire dense and complex network of social inter-action in which I had lived over the past few years, almost without being aware of it, began to crumble. Here, too, there was no "leap"; and this is a pity, because there is no longer a symbolic moment in which a com-munity, however informal it may have been, breaks apart and each of its members joins another community, like the big graduation dinner.

In other words, there was no chance to grieve for those lost friends. Maybe that is why they are ghosts rather than dead.

Not long ago I ran into Mario in a trattoria.

The fact that I ran into him in a trattoria, of all places, stunned me, left me in such a state of amazement, that it allowed the strange conversation that ensued.

Because, in fact, ever since I began living the odd life that I lead, and it became important—essential—to avoid meeting the people I used to know, I have devoted a special attention to trattorias. And by this, I mean the selection of trattorias. Because the trattoria is the most dangerous place there is, without a doubt. When you go to a café, you just take a quick look around inside, and even if someone were to enter after you are already at the counter, you are only there for two minutes, which can be wiled away with two or three phrases of the emptiest formality. At the movies, you only need to sit toward the front of the hall and read a newspaper during intermission. On the trolley, it is a real pain in the neck, because "Nice to see you, what a pity, I am getting off at the next stop" is the only solution. On the train, it's more complex, as "the next stop" might be two hundred miles away, and so you have to take trains that make lots of stops and be ready to get off if everything else ("I left my baggage in another compartment"; "I have to go use the restroom") fails. And finding yourself standing like a dickhead on the platform at Chiusi-Terontola is certainly not much fun.

On the street, all that is needed is a hasty hello and the general attitude of someone late for a meeting. And it is unbelievable how often you run into people. As long as you have no reason to avoid it, you don't really notice. The world is a small place, the idiots like to say, and it's not like they're all that wrong—the idiots—after all.

But the worst place of all, as I was saying, is the trattoria.

There too, of course, you have to take a look around inside before you go in; but if you have already taken a table, and even ordered your pasta, your main course, your side dish, and the fruit, and then someone you know comes in, you are in deep trouble. You can't just leave, and not just because of the waiter and the face he would make, but because the people from "before" are capable of imagining, guessing, suspecting, and a sudden panicky exit, leaving behind a steaming plate of perfectly good food, would be tantamount to a confession.

On the other hand, you can hardly refrain entirely from going to trattorias when you live alone. Every so often, you have to go out and eat a meal. It is practically a physical necessity. Anyone who thinks that eating alone in a trattoria is dreary doesn't know just how dreary a long succession of canned foods and fried eggs can be. I know of comrades who, in conditions similar to my own, have developed cooking as a hobby. That's not for me, maybe because of my upbringing and the fact that I was raised in a bourgeois household where cooking was the mother's job—the stove was her place and her place alone.

And so the trattoria becomes a necessity.

I have pondered at great length which trattorias are the least "dangerous," or even completely "safe." And I have reached the conclusion that—from my point of view—the only entirely safe trattorias are the totally nondescript ones, trattorias that would be impossible to classify in any special way, so anonymous do they appear.

The "comradely" trattorias are the first to avoid, for obvious reasons. Trattorias that are generally thought to "serve good food" should also be avoided. There was a time when it would have been enough to stay away from the "cheap and good" trattorias, but lately it seems to me that a number of comrades are willing, maybe only every so often, to spend a lot of money to eat well. Or maybe it means that the so-called comrades now have lots of money to spend, or maybe this too is just a form of backlash. The result is that—even if I had the money to eat there—I have to rule out the "expensive and good" trattorias, too. Nor can you rely on the "exotic" trattorias. They are considered places for tourists and knuckleheads, but then, when you least expect it, there arises a fad for Chinese, Vietnamese, or Arab restaurants.

Or even Greek restaurants. And if, like me, you are out of the loop, it is hard to tell what the latest fad might be.

And it might seem odd, but even "family" and "neighborhood" trattorias are dangerous; comrades would never go there with their girlfriend or their pals, but they might go from time to time with their parents—who knows?—for a big Sunday lunch (and, by the way, Sunday is an especially dangerous day to eat in a trattoria; with all the stores closed, people might go anywhere).

And so, the safest trattorias are those that are absolutely and completely nondescript. There, you might say, comrades never set foot.

And you know what? You find that there are lots and lots of trattorias like that. It is just another aspect of reality that, in normal conditions, entirely escapes notice. Think of a neighborhood that you know very well, and try to remember the trattorias. You might think of three, four, or ten, and for each of them, you might be able to come up with an adjective, or a number of adjectives. Then go look. There are actually twice as many, three times as many as you guessed, and you had never noticed them at all. Okay, but who eats in these trattorias? Sometimes I think that, when it's all over, I would like to get a degree in sociology, with a doctoral thesis on *Nondescript Trattorias and Their Clientele*. It would be an interesting study because a part of that clientele is, so to speak, obvious—soldiers, travelers who don't know any better, or people who are just in a hurry and want a bite to eat—while another part is mysterious and disquieting, people that, no matter how hard you try, you just can't place. And then, the couples: Who could they be, and why are they there? Secret lovers? In a neighborhood where no one can recognize them? Actually, I don't even know why I went on like this about trattorias, maybe just to explain why I was so amazed by this chance meeting but also because, when you spend a lot of time alone, you develop certain obsessions, certain hobbyhorses, and for me the trattoria, or rather the "theory of trattorias," is one of those hobbyhorses. In any case, this was an absolutely nondescript trattoria; and yet I was just tucking into my spaghetti when I heard:

"Hey, look who's here! Haven't seen you in a while!"

It was Mario, and I was screwed.

I looked up, and there he stood. The same face; the same relaxed manner, with just a hint of irony; the eyes that seemed to "look deep inside you," but without malice.

"Oh, hey . . . " I answered halfheartedly, one last futile effort to ward him off; or maybe it was just a sop to my conscience, so that I could say—to myself, above all—"I did what I could to avoid this meeting."

The next thing he should have said was "Can I sit down?" But he didn't. He just sat down without asking. At the time, I didn't understand; I continued to feel scared and anxious, dreading the conversation that was about to ensue. But then, thinking back on it, I saw the signal that he had tried to send me: you don't ask an old friend, a comrade, "Can I sit down?" even if two or three years have passed, because *certainly, nothing has changed, right?*

Yes, a signal. Because he knew. I mean, he guessed, he

suspected and something more than suspected. But he also knew he was not supposed to know. He knew that in order to talk to me, we had—we were damnably obliged—to pretend, both of us, he that he didn't know, and I not to know that he knew, under penalty (at least in theory) of death, for one of us. And he felt like talking to me, and I felt like talking to him.

"What do you recommend?" he asked.

I had nothing to recommend; this was the first time I was eating in that trattoria, and certainly the last. And in a place like that. . . .

"I thought about you the other day," he went on, "when I saw a movie, what was it called? You know the movie about the aircraft carrier that vanishes and goes back in time, and it comes out at Pearl Harbor, and history could have changed. Funny movie, I mean a piece of crap, but funny. Well, who knows why, it made me think about us, about the old days, and imagine what we would have done if we had been able to travel—still ourselves, no different—a hundred years backward in time, or fifty years forward. Fifty years forward is too complicated, it becomes science fiction. But a hundred years backward. . . . Like, in the days of the earliest Leagues, the first Socialists. I mean, we would have understood that it would take *at the very least* a hundred years, and then to what? Or we would have chosen not to, or been unable to, understand; and in the face of that loneliness, the fact that there were so desperately few of us, what might we have thought or done?"

I could do nothing but listen. What could I say about his loopy rantings? He really hadn't changed at all: the same way of thinking, in depth and in vain, too often focusing on distant matters or pointless events; the same almost morbid curiosity for the thousands of little rivulets of possibility alongside a poorly concealed contempt for reality.

Perhaps I just stopped listening when he asked, "What do you think?"

And maybe that is why—because, for an instant, I had lost control of the situation, and was wandering back in time in my imagination and my memories—I wanted to tell him exactly what I really thought: that I couldn't care less about all this nonsense, that he could take his Socialists and his aircraft carriers and shove them up his ass, and that as far as I was concerned it was enough to be left alone to eat in peace in a nameless trattoria without throwing a whole carload of other shit onto the fire. But, fortunately, he never let me get a word in edgewise.

"Have you ever seen that show on television, around seven o'clock, I think it's called *The Smith Family*? It's not being broadcast anymore, but there are lots of shows like it, I mean normal families who do normal things, with a tiny normal dose of adventure and even drama sometimes. Every time I see that kind of stuff, it has a strange effect on me: I mean to say, even though I know it's a load of crap, it draws me in, it affects me; and it breaks my heart, because you can't help but wonder the whole time you're watching it, 'What are they living for, my God, what for?'; except you can no longer act as if—or at least I can no longer act as if—the question is only about them, because they live one way and not another."

And he was off. Even when his pasta came, that

couldn't stop him. He would talk and eat, eat and talk. And I was caught between the pleasure of avoiding the effort of carefully choosing finely calibrated words and my anger at his pointless chatter; it almost seemed as if he was doing it on purpose.

"It's like certain days that have a special taste and smell, I don't know if you understand what I mean, and you remember when you sensed them for the first time, and you remember yourself back then, and you say to yourself, 'What has happened in the meanwhile, what's changed? Maybe nothing, but do children nowadays feel the same things? Yet that won't save them from becoming adults, like us, will it?' "

But all his questions were rhetorical, or at least he didn't expect any answers. And so I was free to think. Like the thing about tastes and smells, which for me were old songs on the radio, each one a different age, and often tied to a specific moment: this song, sixteen years old and a holiday in Rimini (except not Rimini, obviously); that other song, very young, at nursery school—or could it already have been elementary school—and so on. And as he went on, I got angrier and angrier. What need was there to talk about those things, after we hadn't seen each other for years and everything that had happened? Since even when you are by yourself, you do everything you can not to think about it, I mean.

"How are you doing?" he asked suddenly, right in the middle of another relentless speech.

"Oh, you know, life as usual . . . " I started to say. He cut me off immediately.

"No, I mean your food. How is it?"

It was incredibly bad.

It was not until later, as I wandered through that neighborhood, largely unfamiliar, with its special Sunday sadness, that his pointless blather suddenly seemed important to me, and I tried to remember it.

But it had all been so jumbled and sprawling. Only at the end, as we were saying good-bye, had he seemed to emerge from his delirium and speak seriously.

"We'll run into each other again, I'm sure of it," he had said, just because that is what you are supposed to say. A ghost.

Not long afterward, my work in the organization took an upward turn. They decided (who they were, I did not know at the time) that I had become sufficiently well versed in the sector to which I was assigned that I could graduate to the study of a specific objective, in other words, a major factory, and focus in particular on the relations between labor and management structure.

With this end in view, I was put in touch with another comrade in the organization who was a worker in the factory in question. I worked with him for a few months.

I must say that—perhaps for generational reasons—I had never had big problems in my relationship with the working class. I had never fantasized about it as that obscure object of desire that it was, and often still is, for many comrades who date back to the year of 1968.

"My" working class consisted of the young people whom you met in the Youth Groups and the general milieu of the Autonomia, for the most part identical with students, "layabouts," "druggies" (often because they were also students, layabouts, and druggies), entirely similar to them in every detail (except for the calluses on their hands, as my grandmother would have put it).

This comrade, let's call him Fabio, was something else entirely. He was certainly not the mythical factory worker with a Communist heart, needing only leadership and awareness; he was unquestionably better versed than I was in the new *culture* that by this point I considered my own culture, and he also had acquired greater authority in my eyes through a long clandestine militancy, entirely "in the field," at the cost of enormous personal risk. At the same time, I sensed a "difference"—against which I struggled at length, before finally resigning myself to accept it—that I had never noticed before. Perhaps it was a question of age (he was a "grown-up"), and therefore the differences in our own personal histories, but all that we had in common, was our point of arrival.

What I noticed in particular was his absolute lack of interest in so-called personal conversation—which is *not* a typical characteristic of clandestine militants, nor was it, in his case, a result of his showing caution toward a "new arrival." Before long, I knew where he lived, and at times I might speak on the phone with his wife or children, but he never spoke to me *about* his wife or children.

Still, the work he did was amazing. He knew that factory wall by wall, machine by machine, man by man; and if the work we were doing together required a piece of information that he did not have at his fingertips, he would obtain it with a speed and precision that I found—and still find—unbelievable.

In my mind, I was sketching a map of that factory, with all its countless (and monstrous) aspects. When we were done, I knew *everything*. Everything, everything, absolutely everything. And yet I had never seen it, except from a distance. From far off I had seen it, but never from up close. And as long as the project was under way, I was not supposed to approach it. Come to think of it, I never got close to the factory, even afterward.

Fabio, my "eyes" in that project, was eliminated recently.

And that is just one more thing they will have to pay for. Even though, all things considered, I never liked him much. But *truly* a "good comrade," a phrase that perhaps was developed for people that are not too likable.

Some time after that Saturday at her parents' apartment, I went to the seaside with Anna. But it was nothing serious.

I was supposed to meet somebody, for the first time somebody outside of the usual group of three or four people I knew. Nothing important, just to deliver an envelope.

Traveling with a girl was in any case "better security," and that is how I explained to the organization the fact that I was traveling with her.

I was beginning to sense, through hints and observations, how unwelcome my relationship with Anna—so strange and irregular—was to the organization.

It was becoming increasingly clear that I was faced with a choice: either she had to become involved, or else we had to break up. Bringing her into the organization was out of the question; leaving Anna entirely was something I preferred not to think about. This trip to the coast could be a way of finding a solution.

Her parents had a house on the coast, on the Riviera di Ponente. A house that I really loved, because it was totally unassuming, one of those houses that are eloquent testimony to several generations of prosperity. An old house, practically a cottage, flat and compact, with a dense and luxuriant garden, close to the sea. One of those gardens that you can immediately see was not carved out, square foot by square foot, by the real estate developers. It stretches out, in fact, in a perfectly normal manner, following the terrain with its bumps and slopes, while all the neighboring gardens are level or terraced, organized so as to take maximum advantage of every square inch of land purchased at exorbitant prices.

When we were younger, we had studied for our high school graduation exams in that garden, with the house officially made available to us by her oh-so-democratic parents. Democratic, yes, but not so blind as to let us go there alone. We were accompanied by three of our friends, while her aunt came down from Genoa every other day. But in that garden I had read Tolstoy, and that garden had become for me the site of my version of Russia. I have the impression that I had already heard *The Kreutzer Sonata* somewhere else, in my life, under the bougainvilleas. I know that there are no bougainvilleas in Russia, but a garden is something more than a collection of plants. It is a place that has vanished from our lives. As a little boy, there were no gardens, no yards, in my life. And so I had borrowed for my memories—memories that didn't belong to me—Anna's garden.

I want to try to describe that garden, because even now I think back on it sometimes. The thing that I found particularly intriguing about it was the fact that it was surrounded by netting, a kind of netting that I have seen quite often in the country, with slanting squares of meshwork, draped across the tops of wooden poles and held in place by nails that were clawed down. That netting made me think of foxes. A fox could dig deep enough under the edges of the netting to wiggle underneath and then get into the garden. One characteristic of this kind of netting, in fact, is that the edges become loose. You can get under them and lift them: "That is how foxes make their way into henhouses," I thought to myself.

And the upper edges of the netting also tend to sag a bit. And at the upper edge you could see another typical effect of netting. It would sag under the weight of the bellflowers and ivies and all the other types of creepers that you find in gardens. Bellflowers are my personal favorites. And they are old-fashioned and very rustic, just like foxes and henhouses. And they have this strange way of existing. They need water in large amounts; in the evening, they close up and become a kind of withered tubelet, but in the morning, when it is cool and moist, they bloom again, the same flowers, not new ones, with a pinkish-violet color or a deep dark blue that fades at the base of the calyx. They wither if they are touched, they wither if the sun is too hot; they collapse entirely, heartbreakingly, if they get too little water. Everything seems to indicate that they are delicate, languid plants. And then, when you get to know them, you discover that there is no way to uproot them. They spring up if so much as a single seed hits the ground. And they grow with a frightening voraciousness. From every seed, a stalk springs up; from every stalk, lots and lots of branches. They grow an inch—or inches—a day, and you can actually see them growing. In a few days, they are a shrub, a welter, an impenetrable tangle, that clings to everything in sight, including other plants, even rose bushes. I watched them, fascinated, as they grew before my eyes, so diabolical in their hungry candor, in their insidious delicacy. But I loved them. Their dual nature fascinated me. One day I decided to challenge them. I took a pair of garden shears and chopped them all off at the base.

And for a few days, for a little while, I looked at that empty netting. But only for a short while. Soon they were blooming again, creeping relentlessly upward. And I laughed and gave in. It seemed like a good omen, for me, my life, and my choices.

And so the trip that weekend was for me a happy wish come true. It seemed as if the time when we were studying for our high school exams and my struggle with the bellflowers was something out of the far distant past.

But when something has changed, you can't get it back.

My appointment was for Sunday morning in a bar, in one of those horrible marble-lined squares that are so typical of that city. I had tried to change the appointment because on a Sunday morning it would be difficult to get away from Anna in a place where everyone was everyone else's friend and when all the stores were closed. But it was impossible.

And so the thought of what I was going to say to her was never absent from my mind for the entire two-hour drive along the highway to the sea, with the latest record by Guccini playing endlessly on the tape deck.

Anna was very happy. She had clearly also decided to forget about the last few weeks, so weird, jerky, nervous. We talked about things other than politics. The latest book by Philip Roth, the latest book by John le Carré, *The Honourable Schoolboy*. "What I like best about the book is that in the end there is no enemy," she was saying. "What is an enemy, after all, but something you create inside yourself? Or at least, it is true that the simple presence of an obstacle, a contrasting force, is not enough to constitute an enemy.

"With a contrasting force, you can choose to react in many different ways. You may choose to defeat it by devoting yourself to other things, so as to create the conditions to eliminate its negative weight; for instance, you can create a void around it. Or you can respond with love. There are times when love is by itself a way of reconciling conflict. The way it is between men and women. Or you can simply submit and wait on the riverbank, because it is true that often historical conditions change."

I could feel a wave of annoyance growing in me, already turning into irritation. "An enemy, in order to be an enemy, also needs an active declaration of hostilities from you. An enemy, I mean to say, is an enemy only if you decide to fight him." I could tell, oh I could tell, that she was lecturing me. My nervousness and desire, which were basically a result of my wish to be with her, began to turn against her. What did she want from me, what did she want? Why couldn't she leave me in peace? Was she acting like my mother, who would talk about my hair to tell me what she thought about my grades at school? What did she want? But she was as implacable as always. "Otherwise, why was there twenty years of Fascism, why did it take so long for there to be any active Resistance movement? An enemy is something more than a hostile presence. In your enemy you always find your own obsessions, your own ghosts."

"What the fuck do you want? Do you want to become a member of the Communist Party, or the Christian Democrats? Do you want us to stand around talking about creating a void around—who? Around who? Or do you think that if the Communists gain power they can do anything to undermine the power of the Christian Democrats? And while you're at it, why don't you start with the crap about computers and science, how we should all study so that we can gain control of the means of production?" I was suddenly shouting at her, perhaps just as a reaction to my own insecurities, my anger, because I didn't understand my own state of mind. But what could I tell her? Come underground and live with me under false names? Join our struggle? Yet what right did she have to preach all this crap to me? I continued to answer her, my voice growing louder and louder, doing less and less to rein in my anger and my scorn. "And what about the police shooting at demonstrators, comrades dying, and the illegal labor market? Are these my own creations, as you women say?" But with all my savagery I couldn't shake her self-control.

She responded with silence. I kept yelling, until finally even I felt foolish with all my clichéd phrases, and I shut up. Until we got to the coast, we just listened to Guccini, over and over. That evening, we didn't make love; not until the next morning, a habit that we had developed from waking up together in the same bed in a house all to ourselves; and the habit of having coffee in bed together brought us a little peace.

But the worst was yet to come.

The tense atmosphere of the day before had prevented me from coming up with an excuse. And so the next morning I had no choice: I suggested to Anna that we take a spin in the city and there I would walk into the bar and pretend that I had run into the person I had to meet by pure chance.

"Why don't we go to the seaside?" asked Anna, irritating as always. By this point, I was seeing hidden meanings in everything she said. We got in the car and I started to drive around in absurd circles, trying to stay calm. I went past the bar over and over again, but there was no place to park because on Sunday mornings that bar was frequented by the young smart set. I parked the car some distance away and Anna started to get out of the car to come with me.

"No, please, let me just run and do something," I practically shouted.

"But why? I'll come too, I'll have a cup of coffee." And, increasingly childish and irritable, I answered, "But too much coffee is bad for you."

"Excuse me, but what do you care if I drink coffee or not?"

"Look, just wait for me a second while I go make a phone call."

"Who are you phoning, if we agreed that we aren't going to see anybody?" Anna asked, insistently, her face grave. I was increasingly certain that at this point she had begun to suspect something.

There I stood, fuming, holding the car door open. "Look, it's a long-distance phone call. Do you really have to stick your nose into my business?" She was suddenly cold and distant. "Fine. I don't want a cup of coffee anyway. I'll go take a walk and come back. That way, you can do whatever you need to do."

We walked off, me in one direction, her in the other.

I turned for a moment. "Anna," I tried calling her name.

She must have heard me, but she kept walking.

There was nothing more I could do. If I needed any more proof, those two days were plenty. It had to end. I needed total complicity. And Anna couldn't give me that.

When we knew everything we needed to know about that factory, literally everything, the time came for a new step forward in my work, this time a substantial one. Knowing everything about a factory means that you are ready to identify the critical points, the fundamental people, the strategic nodes in the command structure. They could be considered potential targets: because they are the ones that *it makes sense to hit*. Certainly, this is something that I understood only a little at a time; choosing targets is a very complex process which begins deep down, with a *political* analysis. There is a reason to focus on one economic sector rather than another, factories rather than universities or the army, this factory rather than some other factory, certain individuals in that factory rather than others. And of course there also has to be a correlation between the choice of a target and the "state of organization"; and so there are targets of "routine administration," targets that represent "qualitative leaps," "defensive" targets, and so on.

Now, however, I also understand that contingent factors enter into the process as well.

And so sometimes you choose a target, and specifically a person, because their face made an impression on you the first time you took a hurried survey of the factory. At times, it may be a memory that surfaces, or an internal hierarchy that developed long ago, so that maybe you have a special hatred for people who wear certain clothes, or for that factory where you first leafleted, or for a certain place close to where they killed that comrade. Are these irrelevant reasons? And why? Because hatred is not in the final analysis *political*? Many people say that to us. Many say it in a certain sector, outside of the fighting groups—the twerps who chatter on about human life and pacification in all its various forms, from the humanism of Lotta Continua to the politicos of Potere Operaio.[14] But I don't even take that nonsense into consideration. The ridiculous thing, in my opinion, is that there are even many people in our group who claim that you shouldn't hate the people you attack, because we aren't acting for "personal" reasons but out of a necessary and dutiful opposition to the current state of things. These are the various

Portrait of a younger Giulio Andreotti, seven times prime minister of Italy; it is no accident that when Giorgio and his comrades "liberate" clothing at a *jeanseria*, they tell the owners to "send the bill to Andreotti."Jocularly known to leftists as Beelzebub, he was thought by many on the radical left to be the puppet-master of Italian politics. He was recently convicted on appeal of ordering the murder of an Italian journalist.

above: The lobby of the farmer's bank in Piazza Fontana after the bombing of December 12, 1969. The bomb, which killed eighteen and injured almost ninety, set off a dark succession of bloody events that lasted for decades. The latest—possibly not the last—verdict in the case was handed down nearly thirty years after the bombing.

left: Few images capture the devastation of the Piazza Fontana bombing as do these hats, piled on a bank counter in the aftermath. The Banca Nazionale d'Agricoltura was a farmers' bank, and Friday afternoon, when the bombing occurred, was Market Day, an especially busy time.

In a reenactment of the "accidental death of an anarchist", a mannequin is tossed from the fifth floor window. It is possible to see the height of the railing against which the two men are leaning. The anarchist actually hit the cornice on his way down, suggesting he slithered rather than leapt.

L'Espresso

I guerriglieri

CHI SONO,
COME
COMBATTONO,
COME VENGONO
COMBATTUTI

INSERTO/MANUALE DEL
BUON GIARDINIERE
di IPPOLITO PIZZETTI

This issue of *L'Espresso* appeared shortly after the demonstration that Giorgio described, in May of 1977. The headlines read: "The guerrillas: who they are, how they fight, how to fight them." The picture shows two "autonomi" shooting at the police. The one shooting may be holding his pistol so high because of recoil.

This famous cover layout appeared in late July of 1977; the headline reads "Kidnapping, Extortion, Street Crime: Vacationland Italy." It appeared around the same time that Giorgio became an official member of a terrorist organization.

above: View of the roof of the Bologna train station following the bombing that killed 86 on August 2, 1980, at 10:25 in the morning. The clock at the site of the explosion stopped at that time. It remains at that time even now, 22 years later.

above: The body of Salvo Lima, Andreotti's lieutenant in Sicily, killed in a Mafia attack in 1992, on the eve of a major election. His murder was widely viewed as a warning to an uncooperative Andreotti.

opposite: Leonardo Marino—informer, witness for the prosecution, and confessed accomplice to the murder of Police Detective Luigi Calabresi (who was in turn widely considered responsible for the "accidental" death of the anarchist)—during the trial in which his testimony sent three men to prison for 22 years each. Eloquent body language, typical of his strange, morose testimony.

Flowers adorn a twisted guardrail on the site of the 1992 killing of Judge Giovanni Falcone, his wife, and his bodyguards. Nearly a ton of high explosives was detonated under the highway; one of the cars was catapulted into a nearby olive grove.

"machine-gun professors." And I, who personally abandoned my life as a civilian when I was still a university student, I especially hate professors, wherever I find them.

So, I am emotionally involved, and very much so, in everything I do. And I want, I absolutely want, to have a reason that resonates deep down inside me if I am getting ready to attack someone or to rob a bank. Because I have only one life, and I will only live it once. I am not taking out any mortgages on eternity. My gun is, I hope, something that will serve humanity at large. But in the meanwhile, this is also my rebellion, my hatred, my revolution, just as the path that led me to take up this gun was my own path.

That may not make me a perfect professional revolutionary, a model militant. I don't have the passionless certainty that is required. Let's be perfectly clear, I have never done anything "unprofessional" in all these years; I haven't made any mistakes. And yet some aspect of all this—the fact that I take things personally—always shines through. There is no state of life as transparent as living underground. It is a highly unnatural way to live, rigidly regulated and constantly required to contain a meaning, and it winds up being reduced to the bone in terms of experience. Nothing happens in a natural manner, there is nothing light or easy, because there is no room for things to process themselves in a normal way. Everything is deliberate, everything is chosen. And that is why there are those who shy away from me (I am talking about a subtle thing, not a question of trust or anything like that). But that is also why I never entered what I call the "Soviet" wing of the armed struggle. My sense of life and theirs, my determination to be entirely present in everything that I do, is what separates us. And for that matter, these are the roots of my culture and my decision to take up the armed struggle. This is the thread that leads from the Youth Group right up to the way I am today, and it has never snapped.

I realize that I have gone off topic, as they would say back in school. At the time, the only thing that mattered to me was that I was going into action. It had been decided that one of the potential targets would be entrusted to me. And that was not all. I would have to move for a certain period to another city. Now, I realize that this is not obvious to anyone who has not spent months reading *Il Sole/24 Ore* on a daily basis, but this is how it is. One of the people that our analysis of the factory had allowed us to identify as a crucial potential target actually worked far, far away.

So I was leaving, and I was happy about it. And my role in the organization was becoming increasingly solid and significant. I met other comrades, from my own city and from the city where I would be going to work; and for the first time I was truly living as a clandestine, and for the first time I was working armed, though strictly as a precaution. And so I left, and there began my strange symbiosis with Engineer Caretto.

Our victims, as they are called, often have lives that are less than squeaky clean. The most common thing that we discover while shadowing them is that they have a lover.

Shadowing somebody is fascinating in certain ways.

First of all, it is a true violation of the rules of civil coexistence. Bit by bit, a person is stripped of their private existence. Bit by bit, you wind up knowing everything about a person, and the person never knows it. For example, you wind up knowing all their clothing, their ties, their briefcases and bags, the way their face looks in the morning.

Not everybody that you follow winds up becoming a victim. Shadowing is a way of learning and understanding.

Engineer Caretto, for instance, never became a victim. Among other things, because of his private life.

The city that I was assigned to travel to was beautiful and entirely unfamiliar to me. No cars, no roads. Water that follows you everywhere. I would never have gone there on my own. But in my time underground I spent a very enjoyable period there.

I set up housekeeping in an apartment with a tiny balcony, surrounded by a sea of roofs. Inside, there was a level of luxury that I could not have imagined: wall-to-wall carpeting, a big television set, and bookshelves crowded with science fiction and mysteries.

It was an apartment that belonged to an American, who had unwittingly rented it to us. In exchange, I was supposed to water the flowers every evening and feed a cat that lived on its own, but still showed up every day to eat, on the roof at the edge of the balcony. I lived in a giant comic book of Corto Maltese.

For the neighbors, I had decided to play the role of a student, and every morning I would leave early, staying away until evening. I spent the day involved in a complex, but very enjoyable, series of travels.

Engineer Caretto lived in Mestre, but we had decided that it would be better for me to live in Venice, which was busier and more crowded. So every morning I would go to Mestre and start work a few minutes before the Engineer.

He had a very likable appearance. I think he must have been around thirty-five years old, and he wore the clothes of a thirty-five-year-old: Clarks shoes, herringbone tweed jacket, corduroy trousers. But most of all, he was likable because he had a full head of hair: black, smooth, heavy, without any of the usual incipient bald patches, always a bit distasteful. I knew he had a wife and two small children. In the morning, he would sometimes walk his daughter to the corner, where the elementary school stood, and then he would go back home, get out his car, and drive off. Other days he would leave early and the little girl would go to school alone.

Sometimes I would see his wife and sometimes I wouldn't, because she would take the little boy to nursery school at different times of day, and then she would go to her teaching job. The combination of schedules and children made the times that they left in the morning very complicated and, it seemed to me, very difficult to predict.

Things did not look simple.

Which was just fine with me. The longer I had to stay, the happier I was. At first I would wait for him while he was at work, in case he went anywhere else during the day. But the Engineer was very methodical, and he would always leave at the same time.

And so I would go back to Venice and pass the time wandering around or reading a book on the steps of the many churches in the countless squares of the city.

I had even made some friends, if you can use that term to describe the vendors of peanuts and souvenirs or the people who ran concession stands. We would chat about the weather, politics, Japanese tourists. During one of these footloose days, I practically had a heart attack. I was sitting at a little outdoor café that had already set up umbrellas over the outdoor tables, enjoying a Martini aperitif, and admiring the canal and the bridge and the boats, when I was certain that I saw Engineer Caretto go by on the opposite bank. It was nothing more than a glimpse, and he immediately disappeared around the corner. I leapt to my feet, left some money on the table, and hurried after him.

When I reached the corner around which he had vanished, I saw nothing. I was upset and hesitant. I could have been mistaken; I must know dozens if not hundreds of people who dress like him. And yet that full head of black hair seemed unmistakable. I was suddenly seized with an awful sense of anxiety and guilt. To hell with me, the Martini, and this disgusting city where I had settled back to enjoy myself like some tourist. I raced to the vaporetto and went to Mestre, to wait near the Engineer's house. If it had been him, he would come home early from work. But the house was empty and the windows were closed. There were no signs of life. An hour later, Signora Caretto arrived with the children, all pink and sweaty, clearly coming home from the park. And then, punctual as always, at the usual time, the Engineer came home.

I tried my best to believe that I had made a mistake. But I was certain of what I had seen.

The next day, I went back to work with a new determination, waiting for him outside the factory.

Absolutely nothing happened for a week. I settled back into a slightly more relaxed pace. Then, something happened that set off more alarm bells.

The Caretto family on Saturday would do what every family does.

They would stay at home a little longer than other days, and then they would all emerge together: shopping at the supermarket, afternoon with the children, perhaps lunch at the Engineer's parents' house. And from time to time they would go to visit the mother's parents, who lived in another town, on Sunday.

That Saturday Signora Caretto and the children left the house very late, about ten in the morning. They pulled out the car and drove off. And the Engineer?

I waited all day. He came back at five, with the air of somebody who has spent the day working.

This struck me as remarkable. The Engineer had spent a Saturday at the plant, which was something he never did. I decided that I would not let him get away again and that I would start following him in the evenings as well.

In general, the Carettos would go out two evenings a week, leaving the children at home. They would go to see people in Venice, and they would drive there. After leaving their car in the big public parking area, they would generally walk the rest of the way into the city. Nothing formal, as far as I could tell. They wore everyday clothing, and they would go to visit friends who lived in perfectly nice sections of town, though not luxurious.

Shadowing a couple seemed like a ridiculous job. They were both young, and they did what every couple does. Sometimes they would have arguments; sometimes they were very affectionate. The wife was very cute and, as far as I could see, absolutely innocent.

It annoyed me deeply, to tell the truth, to have to follow them as they walked through the city. Venice in the evening is a city that could melt a rock. On spring evenings, there is a slight mist that creates haloes around the streetlights, and the complete silence, with none of the noise you usually hear in other cities, lets sound travel greater distances. At times I could hear their words and laughter. I found it irritating because my job was not to spy on their private moments. From the gardens behind the walls there rose an odd aroma, somewhere between decay and the piercing smell of flowers I had never seen before. These flowers are white and umbrella-shaped, and I never did find out what they are called. But I do know that they are the source of that special smell because one time I was walking past one and I touched it. It is sort of a graveyard smell, but so intense that it almost seemed painful those evenings I spent shadowing a married couple. "What am I doing here?" I would ask myself more and more frequently.

So many fantasies. This Engineer's work was imaginary, everything I thought about this couple was imaginary, and the pain I felt during these evenings was imaginary. What the devil was I doing here, wandering around like an idiot?

I had to get out of this situation. I blamed the city for everything. It may not be much of a literary reference, but Corto Maltese was right. "Enter these courtyards once and you will never be free of them."

My footsteps mingled with theirs. Step by step. I can hear my own footsteps, how strange. I am following them and they are together.

And then, one Saturday, it happened again: the Engineer did not go with the family. I couldn't bring myself to abandon this lead. I can be really hardheaded when I want to, and I had begun to be fascinated by the mystery. This man was very similar to so many friends and acquaintances of mine. The woman also had a familiar face; she always wore shoes with low heels.

And here I was in this strange city, which I would leave as soon as my work was done.

I continued my surveillance, more and more determined.

One evening the Engineer went to Venice alone.

I hoped that I would finally get a clear fix on what was going on. Instead, he went to one of the usual addresses where he had often gone with his wife, a corner house that practically overlooked the Grand Canal. Another dead trail. I was ready to leave, and by this point I had decided to abandon all of my theories and analyses. I waited, purely out of a sense of duty, and then I saw him emerge from the little street door, by now so familiar, with a woman. A petite blond woman, with low-heeled shoes.

They set off and I followed them. They walked normally,

the usual sound of footsteps in the night. The occasional passerby, the usual mist around the streetlights, the usual flowers with their graveyard smell. A bridge, two bridges, three bridges. The route seemed roundabout, but in Venice you can never say since all the streets wind around in an aimless fashion. As they crossed one of these bridges, he reached out and pulled her toward him. She hugged him back. It had been a quick but clearly intimate embrace—especially her response, so quick, with a hint of desperation.

"What a jerk. What a jerk," I kept saying to myself, and everything was suddenly clear as day. Damn me for a fool. It had been so simple. He has a lover. A simple, obvious, idiotic thing.

And then: what a pig, what an imbecile. I started to swear at him, slowly and relentlessly. I wanted to kick at the stupid wrought-iron fences along the canals, just to work off some steam. Damn him and damn me. That's all. He has a lover. That's where he was going on weekends, that's why he would vanish suddenly. Of course, it was all very clear. They work together and they are family friends, too. Everything was normal, entirely customary; and there I was, with my obsession with politics, imagining who knows what.

They kept walking ahead of me, and then they vanished into a house. After a short time, a light went on on the top floor and, after a few more minutes, went off. Two hours later the jerk stepped out of the door. I had waited for him for the last time. I was chilled to the bone, and I definitely did not want to waste another minute on him. I just wanted to leave him there with his stupid routine existence full of wives, lovers, children, furtive weekends, and hasty assignations.

This time I let him go off without following him, for after all, the stupidest thing you can do when taking a lover is to choose one who looks like your wife. Sad, pitiful, disgusting, and unambitious, even in this. If only he had chosen a redhead with a tight skirt with a slit up the side, or a brunette, or a young girl, or an older woman. But no, a family friend who looked exactly like his wife.

But maybe that was what saved his life. When I reported back on what I had learned, it was decided that Engineer Caretto was definitely a man whose habits were too irregular, too unpredictable. This ratcheted him sharply downward in the rankings of potential targets. And so I stopped my work in Venice and returned home.

Once I had decided to leave Anna, I began to take practical steps. The most straightforward and obvious thing, in these cases, is to let on that you are seeing another woman. This creates a sort of literary situation, a sacrifice for love.

I started to call her less often. Still, we went on seeing each other. Every once in a while, instead of every chance we got, like before. When we did see each other, we would do all the things that boyfriends and girlfriends normally do, and which in fact we had almost never done before, obsessed as I had been with politics and my friends.

We would go to the park and buy food for the pigeons; we would go to the movies, and then to nightspots that were popular with the comrades, to listen to music or have a bite to eat.

And I needed to do all this for other reasons as well. I couldn't just disappear suddenly; I needed to act out a sort of progressive disillusionment with politics. These more relaxed settings, this way of seeming more casual and unconcerned, was a perfect foil. The only problem was that, in a sense, going out like this created some mis-understandings, in Anna but in me as well. Instead of breaking us up, it threatened to create a different situa-tion, a situtation that was just as difficult to break off.

I said it before. Anna is a very serious person. She always looks at things directly. In those months I also discovered that she could be determined and could fight for what she cared about. In exactly those few months— during which I was maneuvering to get out of the rela-tionship—we probably had the most grown-up relationship of all the time we spent together.

In contrast with what I expected, my gradual loos-ening of ties did not trigger reactions of anger or wounded pride in her. All that happened was that our relations shifted. The first few times she asked me ques-tions I was evasive. Then, if she couldn't reach me by phone, she would stop trying, and she would wait for me to get in touch with her. And when I did, she never asked a thing, she never made a comment, she spoke as if we had last seen each other the day before. She would show up for our meetings on time, she was always wearing something new, she would talk only about herself, her work, her friends.

For the first time I would answer in the same tones,

because it was essential for me to pretend that I was slowly losing interest in politics.

And so we would float away in splendid conversations that seemed a little pointless, but that I actually found fascinating. Her parents' house, what a jerk that professor is, the problem with her little brother, the latest news about our mutual friends. And fifteen days later we would take up right where we had left off. And she knew lots and lots of amusing gossip.

She never said a word to me about my absences.

I had other problems. When I went to Venice, I told her that I would be out of town for a while. But I didn't tell her when I came back, in part because my situation had changed. Now I was beginning a full-time occupation. And I would be living in an apartment all my own, a secret apartment. I couldn't seem to break things off with her, or find other solutions. So I came up with a remedy that was very dangerous for me. I gave her an address to write to in Rome, telling her that it was an apartment without a phone and that I would call her. A friend of mine in Rome would send her letters on to me; my letters back would follow the same route.

An exceedingly risky solution, which my organization never learned about. Even though the real problem with security is keeping your head clear and your wits about you. Keeping things going with Anna was much more "secure" than breaking up suddenly, going "nuts," and eliminating all my ties.

I have her letters. I don't read them often. In fact, I never read them at all, but I like knowing that they are there. Sooner or later I will have to destroy them, to protect her.

A new period was beginning, a real life underground. And it had its problems. I was leaving home once and for all. The same lie that I had used with Anna worked brilliantly with my parents. I would need to break off ties with my friends from before, but much more drastically now. And then there were personal and political problems. This time, there was a "qualitative leap"; it was clear that the new apartment was an indication of new work to be done.

First of all, there was a political clarification. I was introduced to other members of the organization, at higher levels, and with them I discussed my future work. Or perhaps it was, in a way, a final check. I had no doubts or uncertainties. A vague lurking anguish, perhaps. But my decision was firm.

Among other things, I was given a "salary." Very, very little money, and the occasional gifts I received from my parents always made the difference between scrimping and outright poverty.

In terms of work, I was to continue working on the same project, but I would also be made available for actions being carried out by other sections.

Despite all these changes, I still knew very little about the organization. By now, for example, I knew a fair number of people, but I had never seen any places; that is, anything beside the apartment in which I was living. If I had to meet anyone, they would either come to my apartment or, more often, we would meet in a public place. It was always the others who would contact me and make appointments to meet. Without advance notice. "By chance" you would meet someone on the street who would say to you, "Go to such and such bar" or "Go to this or that park." Sometimes, when you would go there, there would be someone else who would send you to yet another place.

Living underground. Living underground is a lot of work. Often, quite often in fact, an immense amount of work. And there are no two ways about it, it is such hard work because of the whole problem with social relations and interactions. First of all, to say social relations is excessive. It makes it seem like an ideological issue, whereas I am very clear on the fact that it is not ideological in the slightest, but a very concrete matter indeed. A question of body and skin, and nerves and tears. And wishes and desires.

You may immediately think that it is a question of women, but it's not only a question of women, nor is it even primarily a question of women.

That is, you might say, a separate issue, and I will talk about it—if I feel like it—separately. Here, the question is a more general one: life and social interaction. And in this context it is worth telling the story of the *barista*, to illustrate just what I am talking about.

Now, downstairs from my apartment is a little café, or *baretto*. One of the thousands of little cafés of Milan and the surrounding province. A very traditional layout: a smallish room with small tables and a billiards table, a jukebox, and a pinball machine, a pay phone and the swinging door of the toilet. I spend a lot of time there. You might say that, apart from my apartment, I spend more time there than anywhere else. There's the pay phone, and it is a precious and indispensable tool if you know how to use it properly. There's a jukebox, and for someone like me, who is crazy about music, that is a wonderful thing. There is the billiards table, and I'll talk more about this. And then there is the pinball machine, and, without exaggerating, I am a world champion at pinball. So I started to go to this café the way people normally go to the café downstairs from where they live, to have a cappuccino in the morning and maybe a little grappa when it's cold outside. And then, it's not like I spend my days at the café; that is, I didn't used to, though things are different now, as I will explain.

Before, no, I wasn't one of the guys, like so many of my comrades and friends, who spend hour after hour shut up in their little baretto and then complain that there are no places to "aggregate" (as they say in Rome), and so it makes as much sense to aggregate in the baretto. For me, the café has always been an oppressive place, where turning around means trading elbow jabs with your neighbor; where it's always reeking of dirty plates, and sometimes urine, a reek of urine that wafts from the swinging door in the back (which usually doesn't close quite right); where there are always crowds of people who seem to have nothing better to do with their lives; and where you yourself never seem to have anything better to do with your life. And then maybe it has something to do with my upbringing, and with the idea that hanging out in a café is all bound up with the image of the slightly corrupt time-waster, the good-for-nothing (with bad habits) that was such an obsession for my mother. The fact remains that I just started to go to that baretto in the morning to have my cappuccino. Then, as I said, to make phone calls. This was in the first phase of my life underground, when I believed (when I fooled myself into believing) that it was possible to lead a life that, isolated though it might be, was neither secret nor hermetically removed, and that could therefore involve a rich activity of study and reflection (and therefore of political and intellectual growth) and social interaction.

This led me to believe that it was not necessary to waste time at the bar or "be a parasite of the Revolution," as I would say back then. And I was therefore not "obliged" to spend time at the bar. In time I was forced to face reality, and I began to go to the bar quite often, spending hours and hours there every day. I would play billiards only for the sake of studying the players. That is something I have always enjoyed doing, studying people and trying to understand their personalities and lives, hopes and frustrations—and perhaps it deserves a more thorough discussion, because it bears quite directly on important aspects of my life and my work. Pinball, on the other hand, is anything but a "sociological" pursuit; it is quite simply an ancient and deep-rooted passion. It may be that, as psychologists would say, pinball is a playful activity with a major erotic component, given the underlying movement, reminiscent of sexual intercourse (and God knows I need surrogates for sexual activity). Perhaps, too, it is because pinball was a sort of "forbidden fruit"—in the lectures and prohibitions of my mother—and therefore my earliest transgressions were to go to meetings of Potere Operaio and to play pinball in an amusement arcade (and I did both things during the course of the same afternoon). In any case, finding that pinball machine right downstairs from my apartment and having lots and lots of free time on my hands offered me an opportunity to resume intensely my activity as a "pinball professional." Of course, the pinball machine was not the Rolling Stones machine, which I have read about in a few newspaper articles and which is reported to be the most complex and the fastest pinball machine on earth and has even been exhibited during a conference. Maybe it wasn't the Rolling Stones, but it held its own. Lord, could it hold its own. And so, day after day, I spent more and more time in the bar, working that machine. And that is where I made friends with the barista. And that is where the following events took place, the story of which I shall now tell.

That day, I had just finished a game, and I had made a very high score, 800,000 or 900,000 points which, for that pinball machine, was roughly the highest possible score, and in part without thinking and in part because it was a conditioned reflex, I pulled a felt-tip pen out of my pocket and wrote on the side of the machine, along with the other names and scores, my own. This is what I wrote: "P. L. 800,000," or whatever the score had been. P. L. stood for Paolo Lotito, a name that was assigned me for my first alias. Now I couldn't say whether doing so had been clever or careless: clever, because we were always told that it was best to use your alias as naturally as possible, becoming familiar with it, accustomed to the way it sounds and looks; or careless, because, on the other hand, it is a good idea not to use it needlessly, because it is still a false name, and indiscriminate use of a false name might attract attention and curiosity. The fact remains that I felt like writing P. L. 800,000 and I went ahead and did it.

Probably, what really happened is that a childish desire to show off my skill—an elementary exhibitionistic impulse—had won out over all other considerations. But it never crossed my mind what those initials written on the pinball machine suggested. The café attendant, or barista, was close to me—he and I were the only people in the baretto just then—and he had watched everything I did. He looked at me for a minute, and then he asked me for my felt-tip pen. I handed it to him, and without saying a word, he crossed out the P. L. He asked, "What's your name?" I replied, "Paolo," and he wrote "Paolo L. 800,000." I didn't understand; it was as if I intuited something, but I don't know what, and I asked him, "Why did you do that?" And he answered, "Well, you know, if you write P. L. as in Prima Linea,[15] there is a chance that someone might get the wrong idea." That was exactly how he said it—"get the wrong idea"—and I felt like laughing. And then it occurred to me that I *ought* to laugh; that is, that it was a good idea to laugh, that it would be *good cover*. So I laughed. I laughed in an exaggerated, excessive manner. And I realized that the way I laughed sounded false. He—he later told me that his name was Giorgio—looked at me, in confusion. He seemed embarrassed; he moved off, muttering, "It's better this way, I tell you, it's better this way." I left the bar, and walking toward the nearby park, I sat down and thought about what had happened. There were three possibilities. First, it was pure happenstance. The barista was an obsessively cautious character, maybe even a nut, and by sheer chance he had picked on me to vent his mania and his obsession. Or else it was a joke. He was a bit of a jokester, and like so many jokesters, he liked to make fun of the latest things—this time, terrorism; next time, the national soccer championships. Or, my third hypothesis, he really did know something. It was impossible to say what or how, but he knew something.

And so I said to myself, "Let's think carefully," as if it was an experiment, or a final examination. Or a challenge. Let's consider everything carefully: possibilities and odds, ways out and ramifications. A joke. No, he hardly seemed like someone who wanted to joke; he seemed deadly serious, and his expression was grim, if anything. And then, the few times that I had noticed him, or that we had spoken, there had never been the slightest hint of friendliness or humor.

A nut, maybe. There are lots of lunatics just like that, in the most unexpected places, with the least likely faces. And it's easy to misunderstand them. They say strange, unexpected things, on the trolley or on the train or while you are waiting in line to send a telegram. In low, cautious voices they confide to you and you alone enormous terrifying mysteries, exclusive secrets, apocalyptic intentions. And there you are, listening, without the slightest idea of what to do or say. Sometimes, it was explained to me, they can be more than meets the eye—lunatics, but sly ones—and sometimes they may be paid or maneuvered to be exactly that: sly lunatics. Who knows, but something told me that that was not the case with this barista.

Third hypothesis: he knew something. No, that was impossible. I had been living in that apartment and frequenting that café for just a few months, and up till then I had always behaved in the most absolutely cautious fashion. I had never interacted with comrades from the organization. I had never made phone calls except in the most oblique code. I had never left a newspaper or a piece of paper behind that might prove compromising. And so, what was left? Could he have known me *from before*? That damned weakness of mine, the tendency to forget faces!

I went back to the bar and sat on a chair from which I could watch him closely. First of all, his age. He was older than me. Maybe much older. Between thirty and thirty-five, maybe even forty. His face was typical of many Milanese proletarians—hard to say whether it is grim with intelligence or rage; rich with intuition or thirst for revenge. A face that you see on many of the comrades in the organization. And a face that you yourself would like to have, or you would like to grab whoever is lucky enough to have that face in a bear hug. That was the face he had, and till then, actually, I had never noticed it. And now, there he was, watching me out of the corner of his eye as he washed the coffee cups. And the whole time I was trying desperately to remember. I would close my eyes and try to imagine that face of his in a different setting or a different time. A meeting of Potere Operaio or Lotta Continua, or a mass assembly;

or else the bar of the neighborhood where I used to live, or else the Youth Group, or the gym. No good. That was the method; I did my best, but I was getting no results.

Then, suddenly, in a flash, a picture appeared in my mind and I saw him, like in a movie, right next to me. Yes, right next to me. In Via De Amicis, on that May 14. Certainly, back then he had not been wearing the white shirt and big white apron that he had on now. He was wearing dark clothes, I think, and he had a beard, or at least he was unshaven, as best I could remember. Things had gone like this: As we were running away, my friend and I, we turned the very first corner, and I had run smack into a man. I still had my pistol in my hand, and as I barreled into him, I had immediately and instinctively tried to conceal my weapon. We had both lingered for a moment, the way you do in these cases, trying to get untangled, and I realized immediately that he had seen the gun quite clearly but that it failed to produce the slightest reaction on his part. I stood there for an instant, holding my breath, unsure of what to do. Threaten him? Act like nothing had happened? Run away as fast as I could? He had looked at me carefully, as if he were studying me, and I had just stopped—not because I had decided rationally to do so but because my legs had simply stopped moving, making the decision for me—to look at him as well.

Then, too, in those few fractions of a second, I had wondered furiously, who is this? a comrade? a plainclothes policeman? an agent provocateur? a chance passerby?

When I thought about it later, at home, I continued to be baffled. The way he had looked at me, carefully scrutinizing; the unruffled way he had reacted—all made me think that he was somebody who was "involved in some way," and so probably a comrade (strange, though, that I had never seen him before, never even glimpsed his face) or else a police informer. A plainclothes policeman, that I could rule out; he would have reacted differently. And not a chance passerby; he would have been frightened and shown signs of alarm.

Then, when I happened to think back on the episode—afterward—the fact that I had never seen that face in any other context, much less in places where comrades got together, suggested that he must have been an informer. And now, there he was, taciturn and unsmiling, washing the coffee cups in the café downstairs from my apartment. I started to wonder what was the best thing to do. No, there was no question that he had recognized me, and most likely, there could be no doubt that he knew where I lived, too. The street door of my apartment building was too close to the bar to allow me to just start going to have my morning cappuccino in another café and think that ensured my safety.

Now, the rules of clandestine living at this point would have dictated only one course of action: change apartment. But even the strictest rules have to take into account reality and the resources that actually exist, resources that are often entirely inadequate to needs and possibilities. And this explains the many errors, the many instances of carelessness, and the many limitations that checker the history of the armed struggle—to the clear delight of the various Pecchiolis[16] who then exclaim, "Oh, these guys talk and talk and when it comes to it, they aren't capable of doing things for real. Now, we, back in our days. . . ."

As if we didn't study our history and the history of the armed struggle and weren't perfectly aware of the countless mistakes made by anti-Fascists and partisans during the clandestine struggle. The fact remains that I absolutely could not afford to change apartments, because it would have cost millions and millions of lire. In that case, then, my only option was to watch my man with extreme caution.

At the time, I was reading Conrad a lot, and I remember that in my notebook I had transcribed a passage that had struck me as particularly beautiful.

It read:

> "You must be a good swimmer."
> "Yes. I've been in the water practically since nine o'clock. The question for me now is whether I am to let go this ladder and go on swimming till I sink from exhaustion, or to come onboard here."
> I felt this was no mere formula of desperate speech, but a real alternative in the view of a strong soul. I should have gathered from this that he was young; indeed, it is only the young who are ever confronted by such clear issues.

It seemed, as I said, a lovely passage. And not because I felt like I was in a situation where I would have to choose between sinking to the bottom or climbing onboard. Or anything foolish like that. No, I think it was the reference to youth and facing clear issues. Or who knows what else it might have been; perhaps the sound of the words, the imagery. Or maybe it was just that I liked everything Conrad wrote. In any case, I had read the passage in a short story with the amazing title, "The Secret Sharer," and so it was almost instinctive for me to connect that title to the new situation that was developing. That barista became my secret sharer. Now, if I think back on it, already the reversal of roles between me and him in the image that I had of our relationship was probably significant. In the short story, in fact, the secret sharer was the one who—having killed a man—was protected and "abetted" by the ship's captain. Here, in some sense, he was the ship's captain and I was his secret sharer . . . but let's not exaggerate with our psychological analysis. And so, I decided to stay on my toes and try to understand first of all. The guy was really not a talker—entirely the opposite of the traditional police informer—and he seemed to have no intention of becoming my friend. In some sense, this threw me. I was ready to be evasive and reticent, and instead he was the one who was inscrutable. And that is what persuaded me, in the end, that he was no informer. He was too calibrated to be a comrade, too reserved and discreet, and at the same time, too anonymous and indifferent; a comrade who is not in the situation I am in always expounds his ideas—if nothing else, his tastes, his attitudes, his viewpoints. And for that matter, I thought to myself, why should I keep on assuming that my enemies were all idiots? There could be shifts in the tactics employed by the police, a more intelligent use of the instruments they deployed. Why should I assume that all the agents provocateurs had to be like Frate Mitra?[17]

And so I kept on limiting to a minimum our conversation, and I continued to frequent the bar, though I became exceedingly cautious. I no longer made phone calls from the café telephone, except for the most harmless calls. I no longer made appointments at the café, not even the most harmless ones. As a result, I would sometimes have to walk miles before I could find a phone from which I could call in peace; have to make appointments farther and farther from the apartment; and if I was with someone, rigorously have to avoid passing in front of the bar or finding myself in a location where I could be seen from the interior. Things went on like that for months and months. And then the opportunity came to change apartments. In my place a couple of comrades could live in an entirely straightforward way; they had ties to the organization, but they were not combatants. I moved house in one night. And I heaved a sigh of relief the next morning when I went downstairs to have my cappuccino and entered the nearest café. This was a baretto as well. With two telephones and an excellent pinball machine. And behind the counter, a married couple, two tranquil, peaceful old people.

But I had not forgotten my "secret sharer." I would smile sometimes when I remembered the risk I had run, the risk I had fortunately avoided. But his strange face—his face so unlike the face of a policeman—continued to bother me. And so I was actually not so very surprised—perhaps I was not surprised in the slightest—when, one morning, as I opened the *Corriere della Sera* to the Milanese page, I saw a picture of him. Beneath it was written: "Suspected Militant of Prima Linea Arrested in Baggio."

The whole time I continued my studies. At the same time I was entrusted with a new possible target to pursue. And yet, the first time I was actually involved in an action, it was in support of another section. And it was a fiasco, and a personal failure for me.

In spite of what you might think, a bus or a trolley is not a particularly difficult place to hit somebody. In fact, trolleys offer a number of specific advantages. It is totally normal for anyone to board a trolley, and a trolley is so crowded that in the confusion that explodes immediately following the action, you can usually leave undisturbed. Then, too, there are none of the problems you have with a car—with parking, with changing cars, and possible witnesses noting your license plate number.

Let me open a brief parenthesis. Have you ever thought about how many people memorize license plates and car types? Obviously, I had never thought of it before, but then I have been forced to admit that quite often witnesses remember well, quite well indeed. Who these people are that notice and remember cars, I couldn't say. In my opinion, this is a matter of considerable importance. In fact, what it tells me is that people think about nothing when they walk down the street; they just look around with blank expressions, automatically recording the things they see. Otherwise, what should I make of it? That fear has made everyone watchful and observant? Frankly, I cannot believe this is true. Especially because normally there is nothing to call attention to us, especially in the early morning, which is the most common time for this type of action.

Now, Mario arranged for us to meet on the 27 trolley.

The 27 makes exactly forty stops. We got on at two successive stops. In turn, our stops were two stops before the stop at which our target usually boarded the trolley. I got on and stamped my ticket, lingering at the far corner of the rear entrance platform, taking care not to be pushed back so far that I couldn't move forward. Mario got on just after me, a few hundred meters farther along, and came and stood relatively near me on the back platform. He was wearing a dark blue jacket, like a factory worker, while I was wearing a loden. Neither of us had any identifying features—no glasses, no mustaches, no beards. The guy got on two stops farther along.

He was a southerner. He got onboard with that slightly puffed-up demeanor of someone who has eaten greedily, to excess.

This is typical of police detectives. Especially if they are southerners, and they almost all are; they never quite get rid of that expression of amazement of having actually succeeded in escaping from their little village.

With police detectives, the use of the elbow is almost automatic, in both the metaphorical and the literal sense. Have you ever noticed what an innate tendency to shove police detectives have? It is a subtle but persistent activity, constant and relentless. They shove their subordinates; they shove journalists; they shove people who ask questions, people they arrest, colleagues, and any poor soul who happens within range. They shove even when it is not necessary, always managing to find themselves—and always as though it were the product of pure happenstance—on a collision path with someone else. Onboard a bus or a trolley this instinctive activity finally finds full application. A police detective onboard a trolley does not simply climb on and move forward. No, he plows through the crowd—literally, without showing the slightest effort, he simply *clears a path*.

My police detective that day was no exception, and in the increasingly crowded bus he came to a stop directly across from me. Face-to-face. Automatically, I stepped aside, with a carefully calibrated movement that was neither disproportionate nor overly hasty. I simply shifted to a position off to the side, just to make sure that I was no longer looking him straight in the face. Mario began to move slowly closer. This close this soon was absolutely not a good thing. It was supposed to be our job to take up a position, to choose the right distance and time. But his damned relentless elbowing, typical of the poor southern Italian that he was, had brought him face-to-face with me—a very undesirable state of affairs. Now I would need to move slowly away from him; but if I moved away from him, it would be a singular thing for me to move back toward him just a few moments later. He might notice, and he might have an intuition, as sometimes happens; and for that matter, he had every reason to be watchful. And at that point, if things go suddenly wrong, then a bus truly can become a death trap. A death trap for you and for everyone else, because at that point you absolutely have to do something crazy— hold off a crowd of people by waving a gun or even point your gun at the head of the driver or the conductor. But it's not like hijacking an airplane. On a bus any of the passengers can open a window and yell for help or cause trouble in some other way. And the police detective himself might start shooting. It's already happened before, in Rome. And it didn't work out very well for the people who were there.

Mario moved closer with that in mind. We didn't look at each other, but it was clear to each of us what the other was thinking. I quickly considered the possibilities: the simplest thing would be to wait for the next stop and, with the wave of new passengers climbing aboard, allow myself to be shoved a little farther forward, but not too far. From where I stood, I could see him as if I were looking through a magnifying glass. Every so often the trolley would lurch, pushing us in one direction or the other, thrusting us together. I desperately needed to brace myself against the swaying. I did not want to touch him. I didn't want him to brush against me. That, above all else. That could not happen.

And I thought that I could smell the aroma of his aftershave, the smell of the Floïd that barbers slap on in such generous abundance. It was just an impression, actually. There was no odor, but I thought I could smell the reek of his aftershave, and I did not want—I absolutely did not want—that odor to transport me back to the bathroom in his apartment, where he had washed, shaved, taken off his pajamas. I started to be swept by a wave of fear, while he, chubby and unconcerned, let himself sway back and forth, distractedly following the lurches of the bus. I held myself as rigidly as I could, but there is only so much you can do. I was holding myself with my left hand, my left arm. My right hand was holding my pistol in the pocket of my jacket. But that position was no longer enough; or perhaps I should say, that position no longer calmed my nerves. I was swaying too, like a damned soul. Or at least I thought I was. And with every lurch of the trolley, I would break the slight fall toward him with a sharp jerk of my hips. I was no longer paying attention to Mario. I was just waiting stiffly for the next stop, so that I could finally move freely. Of course, I could have moved even then, but it was as if I had fallen into a trance for a moment; or at least, afterward, that is how I recall the sensation of repulsion at the thought of any possible contact with his body.

Then he turned. As so often happens, I saw in his eyes that quick glance that occurs when somebody focuses for an instant on whoever happens to be standing in front of them. Visual processes that you see on trains, in elevators, and of course on buses. He looked at me for a second, registering my presence, and then he sank back into the expression of someone going somewhere else. That slight movement, however, had been enough to free me from the obsessive dread of contact. On the other hand, his quick glance had unleashed in me a feeling of irritation and an irrational wish to pick a fight with him. His stupid gaze, his stomach pressing against his gray uniform, the immense tension of a few seconds before, were all transformed into a blind fury.

I stared straight into his face and began to stare at him fixedly, the way bullies do when they want to start a fist-fight. I stared at him intensely, without managing to lock eyes with his bovine gaze. A string of curses began to form on my lips. It had nothing to do with the pistol that I was holding ready. I repeat, it was just a quarrelsome mood of irritation with his gray outfit and that round face of his.

"How dare you?" I wanted to say. "How dare you? We know every detail of the work you do, of your filthy work as cop and executioner. And you are such a jerk that you don't even have a foreshadowing, a flash, a sense of what's coming. . . ."

The next wave of passengers got on. They pushed him and they pushed me. This was the perfect moment to slide away. Instead, I moved closer, I bumped into him, I pushed into his belly. "Excuse me," I muttered, staring intently straight into his eyes: finally.

Finally, yes, but in the meanwhile, something had happened. He had been able to stare straight into my face; I was now in a totally different position from the plan; Mario was completely thrown off balance by my behavior and my movements, and from the corner of my eye I could see that he was watching me—he looked confused and inquisitive. And then, the smell of Floïd, the big soft belly, the big cowlike eyes, his squalid uniform . . . Good Lord! It was all too much. It swept over me, as if he had tucked me under his arm, as if we were crammed into a crowded elevator. I turned aside suddenly and stepped away. Just then the doors opened and I leapt down, to be greeted by the curses and exclamations of the passengers at this new stop who were trying to board the trolley. Mario got off at the next stop, from the correct door. He, the police detective, was killed months later—possibly by mistake, possibly by members of another cell—aboard the same trolley.

The funny thing is that that time I wasn't even supposed

to shoot. I was only supposed to watch Mario's back, along with, possibly, another person I had never even met. And the result was that I had created a huge problem, almost a disaster. And even though it hardly met with approval—quite the contrary—I have to say that the organization was not too hard on me. There was another meeting, events were discussed in detail, and I was asked, repeatedly, if I felt ready to take part in other armed actions. In all sincerity, I felt I was ready, and I said so. There was also a certain degree of self-criticism on the organization's part for having assigned me for my first action in a sector other than my own and on a target about which I knew nothing. I would concentrate on my own sector, therefore, and that is where I would take part in the next armed action.

The question I ask myself most often is whether I did right or wrong to choose this life. The question that lies closest to my heart, though I ask it only rarely, is whether and how much I have changed. I have been inside this life for a fair number of years now. And it is an unnatural and specific way of living. Has my personality changed, has my way of thinking changed, have I changed physically?

Unfortunately, I cannot say. I can only guess at what I am like. In reality, I don't have anyone with whom I could talk it over. Maybe, in the life I left behind me, talking about yourself occurs so spontaneously—it is so much a part of everyday interaction—that you talk about yourself, you analyze yourself, and you have terms of comparison without even having to wonder about it.

But now, how to do it? I have friends who are in this

situation, but I see them rarely, and when we do get together we speak in the technical, activist jargon involved in the larger question of "what is to be done?" and all of the countless daily steps required for security, survival, and political activity. Personal questions are veiled, as if they were somehow shameful.

And so I have no terms of comparison.

Yet I think I have changed.

Deep down, I think my mother knows something. She has no concrete reason to know anything at all. My version holds together. I am living in Rome. I make my living with odd jobs, but I am pursuing great artistic ambitions. That is not exactly what she had hoped for me, but in some sense it is better now than a couple of years ago when she knew I was involved in the doings of the Youth Group.

So she is less worried, she says. She asks me about money, my apartment, and every once in a while she pisses me off by asking me if I'm taking drugs. She asks these questions on the telephone. When I finally saw her again in person, I sensed a disquiet that seemed new in her and that a few years ago I would not have understood.

Now I understand; I feel she is very close to me, present, intrusive.

There. That is one of the things that has changed. I have more senses, I understand more things. Inside me, there is more room to understand things that I would never have noticed. But there is more.

Now I can *feel* myself.

In the solitude, in the effort, in the doubt of all the experience I have been through over the past few years, I have developed an ability to "feel myself," to watch as I live and therefore, also, to perceive the lives of others.

I have become more sensitive. In some sense, this is an occupational hazard, the result of living in a perpetual state of alert.

But that's not the only thing. Now I have a different kind of "memory," a greater capacity to register things as well as to feel emotions.

I never really loved my mother. There were—and are—so many things about her that annoy me. I am not certain exactly how old she is now. Probably a little over fifty. She's more or less like all the fifty-year-olds of her social class. They are something more than housewives, because they attended university and they had jobs, but with that housewifely way of being emancipated—they worked as teachers. She has gained weight, but she has not let herself go totally to seed. She goes to the beauty parlor, but she continues to have her hair done in that helmet style typical of every other old-fashioned respectable lady. She wears a tailored suit, with jacket and skirt. Every suit the same, for as long as I can remember. Gray with a pleat in the front, black when there was a reception for the parents at school. Black with a little white blouse.

How I hated her and our apartment, where everything was always exactly the same as thousands of other apartments just like it—the living room, the bedroom, the kitchen, a cleaning lady who came twice a week to help the "signora," and my own bedroom where nothing was ever thrown away, not even the rag duck that they gave me for Christmas who knows how many Christmases ago.

Everything was just like it's supposed to be. We even have a little summer house. Or, I should say, a little apartment that I think they are still paying for. Three rooms in a tiny building with four apartments.

We would go—actually, they would go—every August. And of course the apartment is packed with framed artwork made with dried pressed edelweiss blooms and pictures of me as a little boy; in the garden there is a wooden donkey with geraniums drooping from its saddle.

Once I went to visit them there. I took a bus. I got out in the main square of the little town, and I walked all the way uphill to the apartment. I had told them that I would come without specifying exactly when. In reality, I needed to get away for a while, and I needed to reassure my parents.

"I'm coming to stay with you for a week, Mamma. I'll see you when I get there," I told her on the phone.

"Wonderful. When?"

"Mamma, I told you, I don't know when. And what difference does it make to you? You're already there, and at a certain point I'll just show up."

"Of course, of course. All right. It was just so that I could make something special for you, something you like. Air out your room . . . "

"Mamma, don't start with this crap, otherwise I won't come at all. I am calling you long distance and you ask me what I want to eat."

"All right, all right. But don't complain later."

"Oh, come on—"

"Do you want to talk to your father?"

"No, that's okay. Say hi to him for me. I am almost out of coins."

"All right, sweetheart. Take care of yourself, stay well."

"Okay, Mamma, bye bye."

"Oh, wait a second. Remember to bring something for your aunt when you come. This year she is staying with us because she is getting older and she never quite recovered from her fall."

"Mamma, I know, I know. I'm out of coins. We'll talk about it, bye."

That is exactly how exasperating my mother is. I call her on the phone and she asks a lot of useless questions: How will you get there? Do you want to take the bus? What's the weather like in Rome? Did you buy an overcoat with the money I sent you? But for some time now there has been something approaching respect for me in her voice. A way of looking at me—or listening to me, really—with consternation. For example, why does she no longer ask the usual questions with which she has busted my chops for so many years? The question about women, for instance. There are an infinite number of variations on this question, as I learned in my short period of time living with my family. "Where are you going this evening?" Or else, "Who will you see when you go out?" Or, after passing me a phone call, "This friend of yours, she calls quite often, doesn't she?" Always tossed out with nonchalance, while stirring the pot or doing some chore, during the afternoons that I would spend at home (few as they were). Then there's the question "What do you want to be when you grow up?" This too is an intrusive question. Especially because it is one of those questions that more-or-less up-to-date parents think might provoke a reaction. I could see it in her face. On the one hand, she wanted to "know": Does he want to be a professor? a doctor? a lawyer? What the devil does this beloved son want to do, since he never seems happy with anything? But alongside her curiosity, there is also fear. "And what if my question irritates him," she thinks to herself, "and I wind up obtaining the opposite effect, making him cling to his position of rejecting everything?"

And so she would launch into long, wandering circular statements, with which she would try to hint things to me. I could see her suffer. I knew I could help her by just cutting her off and saying, "Mamma, don't bust my chops," or "Say what you mean; what do you want to know?" Instead, I would leave her dangling, embarrassed, awkward. And the less I would say, the more she would become entangled in endless phrases that never went anywhere. They usually involved praise for my cousins who, young though they might be, were already off to excellent beginnings.

She no longer asks that kind of question. And yet she can't be fooling herself that I am doing great things in Rome, like I told her. And she knows that Anna and I have stopped seeing each other. Anna herself told her; she calls her every year to wish her a Merry Christmas.

And in the meanwhile here I am walking up the hill to the apartment, thinking about all these things. When have I ever thought so much about my family? Isn't this, I ask myself, proof of how much I have changed? The little wooden donkey is right there. In the yard, there is a ping-pong table, too. Children I have never seen before, and my aunt. It's true, my aunt—my father's sister—has aged. My God, I hardly recognize her. I really don't remember her looking like this.

Not my mother. She hasn't aged a day. The mask she wears will last for the rest of her life. My father has aged, however. But, come to think of it, why should I bother keeping track of such normal things?

An opportunity for action presented itself quite soon. It didn't take long to select the right target from among those that had been identified. Right in many ways, obviously, ranging from strictly political considerations to the more pedestrian practical issues. This was not the person that I had been "looking after" in the last few months, but it was a person whose position I was familiar with; I had a clear understanding of his role in the corporate structure. In brief, unlike the police detective on the trolley, it was not only possible but easy to consider him an enemy, in part and especially through a logical process.

Because in reality it is not easy to answer the question, apparently so straightforward, of "Who is the Enemy?" The partisans could easily answer the question. The Enemy is the Oppressor. The line between Him and the Others was clear. The difference was even marked by language, German for the Italians, French for the Algerians; or it was made physical by a uniform, a Black Shirt or a uniform. Who the enemy is nowadays is clear to many, in many countries. He may not be the Oppressor. But he is recognizable all the same.

But who is the enemy in Italy, in a so-called democracy constituted by an iron-bound alliance of all the parties; that is to say, with all the weight and determination of the most powerful labor movement in the entire Western world?

Who is the enemy, if he often wears the clothing of a factory worker in your same manufacturing division? And if, even more frequently, he went to school with you and is now in charge, as a left-wing union officer, of the reorganization of the factory on an international level?

So, who is the enemy? Our documents are clumsy, hackneyed, badly written. Often, they read as if we were so many schoolteachers. Or civil engineers. But they are written that way because they have to be. Discussion, analysis, and debate are not simple matters for us, or at least not for me. And so, in reality, there are not only more doubts, but also radically different scenarios. Preparatory tactics that are more homely, more obvious, more everyday. Just as the enemy is no longer the Enemy and no longer has the trappings of power, just so our actions are no longer spectacular and adventuresome. The preparation of an attack in the way we conduct our armed struggle, here and now in Italy, has much more in common with the approach of a scrupulous accountant than that of a guerrilla fighter. It has more to do with accuracy than daring; there is more calculation than courage. In this period, of course, I have been reading a lot. If I had to describe something similar to what I do, I would refer to George Smiley, the head of the secret service in the novels of John le Carré, rather than the secret agents of Ian Fleming. The qualities of Smiley that I have in mind are his anonymity, his great skill at concealment, his capacity to memorize, record, and analyze, especially, details. And so our attacks, the way we prepare, have nothing to do with attacks on armored vehicles or with audacious plans to blow up secret bunkers or entire military platoons.

An attack is prepared first and foremost with solid sensible shoes and a warm overcoat. And the preparation of an attack is by and large a long series of street names, like: Via Rossi, corner of Via Pontaccio, continue along Via Vittorio Emanuele, Bar del Portico, 81, 83, 85bis, apartment 12, 1:45 A.M., 1/17.

I imagine that few wars or guerrilla campaigns or armed uprisings, call it what you like, have required the level of drudge work, routine, or rat race that is so much a part of ours.

No heroes, and no heroics; and dull lives. I might be wrong but, at the risk of repeating myself, no other armed experience seems similar to the one we are conducting today. We are even outdone by the police, in our gray anonymity. At least they can promise: "Join up, and you'll see the world." Here, we see only lots and lots of industrial hinterland.

And I saw a lot of outskirts and outlying areas this time as well. Once we had selected our target, we were all assigned to him, each of us with a different task. Until, once again, we knew everything—absolutely everything—about him. At that point, establishing a plan, deciding how and when we would hit him, was the easy part.

• • •

I don't sleep much.

And that makes me think. Because it is not a matter of anguish, or fear, or insomnia. There are times of course when that can happen, but only when you would expect it, only as much as normal; and even then, less and less as time goes by, as I get used to it, I build up defenses.

What makes me think is something else. The way that it is possible to change habits, ideas, forms of behaviors, ways of life, radically, drastically; and the way that instead you find there are spaces—apparently, spaces that exist somewhere straddling the territories of mind and body—that resist change, that remain apparently unchangable, always the same through time, like archae-ological remains of an impossibly distant past, useless, encumbering, but there they remain. Like for instance this habit of staying up late—a habit that was probably, in part, left over from other times, when I would stay up late drinking, debating, with friends, with girls, and sleep late in the morning; yet the habit remains even when you have to get up early, when the days are long and tiring, and when in the evenings, especially, you have nothing at all to do.

And yet every evening, I say, "I'll go to sleep early tonight," and it seems to me that I need and want to sleep. And then it all goes wrong. I read a newspaper, smoke a cigarette, leaf through a detective novel, listen to music on the radio, think thoughts half-formed and scat-tered, smoke another cigarette, and so on until it's late again, just like last night, just like tomorrow night. . . .

There they are, the boundaries of awareness, of conscious choice, sunk deep in the rhythms of the body. Persistent.

157

It's annoying.

And not just because of how I feel the next day, dragging physically until it seems like I can't get around, can't drag myself from here to the next place. That I can get over.

It's because of the dreams that I get so annoyed. I only manage to dream after many long hours of sleep, in the fitful sleep of the early hours of the morning. At least, the only dreams I can remember.

And I have discovered that dreaming helps. It relaxes me, relieves the tension. In short, the few times that I manage to have a good dream—and a good dream does not necessarily mean a nice, cheerful dream; it just means a long, substantial dream—I wake up feeling relatively cheerful. Not that you think back over your dreams, or analyze them, or anything like that. Even if I did, I wouldn't understand—sure, years ago I read something about Freud and psychoanalysis, like everybody, but nothing more.

It is as if it were a pressure valve, the only release available. And I'm not talking about sex dreams, which can be nice in one way but depressing in another, and in any case are of no use in terms of the tension.

But there are other, horrible dreams, practically nightmares, which all the same make me feel better in the morning.

For instance, this dream. From a couple of days ago.

I was staying with friends, a married couple; they had a little baby, one year old or thereabouts. We were talking. I understood, I knew, somehow—the way it is in dreams, you know—that there was something wrong with the baby, that the air he breathed in he couldn't breathe out; and I saw the baby swell up and swell up, till his body and face were grotesquely deformed; and I thought he would explode. Both I and the parents were horrified, in anguish, but I was especially anxious because I knew that in order to save him I would have to puncture the baby with a huge pin, to let the air escape. It was my responsibility—I don't know why—but I was not sure I could do it, and I was hesitating. The mother was the only one who took action. She went over to the baby and started to strip off its skin. It was strange to see; as if she were *peeling* an orange, that's how the skin came away. But it was no good. The baby kept swelling. And then stopped, all by itself. It had fixed itself, it was all better. But I thought to myself, it could start again any minute; something needed to be done. Then I woke up; or the dream ended.

I never dream about the carabinieri, the police, or that sort of thing.

And this strikes me as weird, too, because I remember, from the old days, when I happened to talk with others about dreams and we would tell each other our dreams, lots of people in the most ordinary, relaxed situations, dream about the police. Who knows why. Maybe it's the fear of punishment that in this miserable society of ours everyone carries around with them; certainly the men in uniform are an excellent way to represent that fear.

But I don't dream about the police. Only once, as far as I can recall. I was driving and a policeman stopped me, pulling out his police signalling disk. The incredible thing is that, in my dream, I was totally unconcerned, and I was thinking to myself, there's no problem, I'm fine, my papers are all in order.

Instead, I dream a lot about doctors, who knows why. Here, too, there is something strange, however, because I never have dreams about violent situations, blood, wounds, operations, surgeons; never medical instruments that cause pain.

Maybe, at the outside, X rays. Once, and that was really a "good" dream, I remember that I dreamt I was riding on a bus, but it was different from the usual layout of a bus, and instead of a ticket-stamping machine, there was an X-ray machine, the kind that you stand up inside of, and in the front you can see inside.

Inside it there was a boy, about ten years old, more or less, and looking at that sort of screen were three or four doctors, all in their white lab coats. After a while, the head doctor, or at least the one who seemed most important, said, "Yes, he's getting better; he may survive." The dream ended there.

We waited for him at the corner, each of us in our disguise; and even though they were ordinary everyday disguises, they struck me as strangely funny. (In reality, they weren't even real disguises, per se; they were camouflage, perhaps I should say, but the fact remained that they struck me as really funny.)

Everything went according to plan; and this time it couldn't have gone otherwise. And yet it was all so quick, simple, almost mechanical, that I couldn't say what I was thinking in those few moments as it happened, and quite possibly I wasn't thinking a thing.

Fear, certainly, lots of fear, but before, while we waited. And it was a fear not unlike the fear you feel before an important exam as you pace nervously in the school hallway. And like the fear before an exam, this fear vanishes magically the instant you enter into action; or else it doesn't vanish, but then it's panic, escape. Afterward, terrible fatigue, a sudden empty purging and relaxation. You could sleep for twenty-four hours without waking up.

In the middle—nothing, or nearly nothing.

He dropped without speaking; nor did we say anything.

Then we moved away quickly.

Since then, I have taken part in other armed actions. But honestly, if anything has changed in me in the meanwhile, if perhaps I am no longer the same person, if I have revised my view of many things about myself, my life, and my ideas, it is not because of this type of experience. Which, if we want to talk about violence, is much less violent, for you and for the victim—for yourself with respect to the "victim"—than many other experiences.

But shooting isn't fun. No, it's not thrilling, like some people think and claim. Maybe it was back at that first big demonstration, but not now, not anymore. It is just, in a sense, logical, inevitable, clean. And rational.

I have thought a lot about the ones who talk. Not about the political judgment: that is obvious; it goes without saying; it is unquestionable. And in terms of operative steps, the treatment that will be meted out to those who talk, at the proper time and place, is equally obvious.

But what remains—or what should remain—is that the real problem with this type of situation is that the obvious conceals the hard-to-understand, certainty overshadows doubt, what needs to be done prevents you from thinking things through. And people ought to think things through, carefully.

As for myself, I often wonder, "Why do they talk?" But I know perfectly well that the real question is "What would I do?"

Let's be clear, there is no shortage of answers. In fact, the real problem is that there are too many answers.

Violence, torture, these of course are the first consideration, and there, quite frankly—rhetoric aside—it is hard to say what I'd do, and so it is hard to judge and condemn. What do I know, what can I say? Nobody can know in advance; it's only in movies, thank God, that they torture you to train you, to test you. I can imagine— if it happened to me, knock on wood—that I would try to kill myself, I think; I'd certainly try not to talk. Who can say?

And in fact—as far as I'm concerned—I don't think that I can condemn those who talk and do nothing more, those who give up, fold. In other words, it's not the "confession" that makes me indignant. It's the question of "repentance," the idea of talking and then justifying it, taking credit for it, that disgusts me; but that is also what I find unsettling. Why it disgusts me is, I think, pretty evident. It is all too clear that the "repentance" is an inescapable component of a deal, that if they are going to give you something, in exchange they are not satisfied with you just talking—they might be able to get that out of you in any case—they also want it to seem spontaneous, voluntary; they want you to betray.

What I find unsettling is that someone, and sometimes these are major figures, should accept; that to some the deal—right then, right there—might seem like a really good deal. Here is what I am trying to say: it seems to me, and I am not alone in this, that the day they catch you, it's all over. I mean over-over; I mean, your life is over. Except for certain possibilities like escape, the Revolution, a miracle. But these exceptions are so exceptional that, leave aside counting on them, even just entertaining the possibility could lead only to madness.

But—and this is where I get really angry—it's that, in any case, I can't understand how anyone can fail to see this, fail to know it. In other words, what's the difference between spending your life in a maximum-security prison and spending your life "free," in Argentina or somewhere like that, the whole time—and I mean the whole time, minute after minute—looking over your shoulder, waiting for the payback, the final settling of accounts. You call that living? Why? Or is it that once they have you, everything changes, and you don't think that way anymore? But why?

One of the things that I think has changed me over the past few years has been the realization that relations among us are terrible. The life we lead does not encourage solidarity, but rather tension, resentment, and constant conflict. My friendship with Piero has been transformed, too. Today, I think there is an exceedingly intricate relationship made up of disquiet and a great deal of rivalry.

Piero's path was different from mine. We both entered the organization at more or less the same time, but he immediately moved to another city and there had in a sense more relations with the circle of comrades, because there were fewer obstacles to social interaction. In that smaller city, in fact, over the past few years, there was a process of continual interaction and exchange between certain political areas and us.

Piero has always led only a semiclandestine life. That is, he did not lead a life, like mine, that was exclusively devoted to military activity, nor was his life as harsh and as lonely as mine. He had external contacts and sufficient cover that he did not need to be alone; he took part in more open and more extensive political activity. He had his women, his friends, his evenings out. His time was not totally ravaged. And deep down, I have never forgiven him for this "privilege" of his. But what he is today is the complete opposite of what I am. The more time he has spent on his own, the more rigid and waspish he has become. I can't think of other words to describe his state of mind, a sort of permanent mental erection. It has become impossible to talk to him. He lectures, he fumes, he makes vibrant speeches, he knows everything and defines everything. He has become one of those people, in other words, that I just can't stand. We lived together for a long period of time when we were preparing for a major attack; a number of us took part, and we went to live in another city for a long time to prepare for it. The attack was not a simple matter. And so we all were living in a challenging situation in psychological terms. You couldn't say that there were fears or doubts. But when you are faced with certain challenges, you need a climate of tranquillity and even affection that was just not there. In fact, the longer this goes on, the less of it there is.

Four of us moved into an apartment together. That was the beginning, for me, of one of the saddest periods of recent years. It's not easy for four people to live together. Aside from Piero, Milanese like me, from my same circle of friends, and the same age as me, there was Beppe, a former university student who comes from the deep, small-town South of Italy and who had been living in Rome for many years. Then there was Giovanna, whose apartment we were living in. Giovanna was the oldest, a serious-minded and very laconic schoolteacher. She was considered very reliable, but I believe that this was her first major action.

Piero and I arrived before Beppe did. It was our job to start scoping out the situation and plan out the attack. Beppe showed up one evening. He was constantly swearing (in time I got used to it): "Fucking screw the Madonna."

In the evenings, we would eat at home. Giovanna did the shopping so that we were not obliged to interact with the local shopkeepers. And she distributed her purchases among various stores so that it was not obvious that she was buying so much more food. The evening that Beppe got there, he telephoned just as the spaghetti was ready to eat. We decided to set some aside and to begin eating without waiting for him.

"Screw the Madonna, this fuckin' hill. It's a good

thing the food is ready, 'cause I am dyin' of hunger here." He dropped his duffel bag on the floor, grabbed a chair, and sat down. The only one he had never met was me. But he didn't bother saying hello. He scarcely acknowledged Piero, though he knew him well, and he gave Giovanna a sort of peck on the cheek. And then: "Fuckin' oatmeal, always fuckin' oatmeal, the pasta you make up here in the north. This spaghetti is absolutely disgusting."

Beppe, I learned in time, was just like that. He complained about everything and he was always starving— for everything; for women and spaghetti, newspapers and time. And he was resentful. Especially resentful of us northerners: "You northerners who always think you have a fucking right to everything. But that's not the way it is. Let's get that straight from the beginning. Fiat came down south to suck our blood, from Cassino to Sicily. The way they always have. And before you know it, we don't even have the right to notice it, to point it out. Even the comrades, even the militants—you better believe it— pour out the usual bullshit about the south. Theorizing and revolutionary holidays. But who is really still there? Who goes there? Who stays there?" After twenty minutes, he was delivering a true stem-winder.

It dawned on me that his real problem was with Piero. Piero acted like he was quite the intellectual. Giovanna continued to do all the chores, behind her usual veil of silence. But when dinner was over, she said sharply, "Boys, your mother isn't doing the housework anymore. Everybody is here now. The only reason I do the shopping is that it's best that way. But this is the first and the last time that I am making dinner for all four of us, and I am not going to wash the dishes and clean up. And I have no intention of allowing this apartment to become a pigsty."

She went into her room. The plates sat on the table until the next day.

The question of the apartment became a perpetual source of conflict among us. I was annoyed by the atmosphere of a student commune. If there was something I was supposed to do, I would do what concerned me and was due from me directly. In other words, I didn't feel like cleaning other people's whiskers out of the sink. Beppe, on the other hand, didn't think there was any reason to be so squeamish. "I've lived in those pigsties they call dormitories. I got used to living in filth because students are filthy." Piero promised he would do his share of chores, and then said that he had forgotten and would do his share the next day. I found this behavior of his especially irritating. In some sense I felt like he was letting me take up the slack—as if he were trying to create a relationship with me in which the old roles were reversed; as if now he was more experienced than me, he had more of a say in things, he was more important. He would impose his conceit on me in subtle ways. Giovanna tended to restrict interactions with the others to a minimum, hovering somewhere between resentment at our presence and friendliness.

Giovanna continued to be a genuine mystery to me. She was respectable and very shy, a creature of habit and ordinary in appearance, introverted and apparently quite sensitive. Now a routine was beginning. The preparation for the attack. Preparatory discussions. The assignment of tasks and roles.

And each of us would accentuate our personalities in the process. Piero would lecture, I would become irritated. Beppe would complain, Giovanna would say nothing. And yet we spent a lot of time together. When I say that there was no solidarity among us, I may be overstating the case slightly. Because, by spending time together, we created the feeling of having something in common.

But there was no feeling of closeness.

And Beppe annoyed the hell out of me. Did I still like Piero? I don't know. Sure, there was still a strong mutual bond. But we never, or rarely, really communicated. We mostly talked about politics and practical matters. We were pretty cheerful together. Sometimes his tossing and turning woke me up at night. But we never discussed that.

"Do you like Giovanna?" I asked him one evening, when we had turned the lights out early and we were both lying awake in our respective beds.

"Not a bit. She sits in the corner like a dog that's been whipped. No, I don't like her. But then I am against this small town stuff, with everybody fucking everybody else. In the period when I constantly had to change apartments, I had a really nice time. There's no woman on earth who will turn down a fugitive from the law," he said, with a hint of laughter in his voice.

So that's it, I thought to myself, Piero has become an obsessive.

"Not me," I said. "I've just gone to a lot of whores."

● ● ●

There are two ways of talking about guns. There are those who worship guns, and there are those who use them without thinking twice about it. There are those who talk about guns relentlessly and there are those who never talk about guns at all. There are those who act like experts and those who barely know how to use them, except when absolutely necessary. Beppe talked about guns endlessly and considered himself to be a major expert; he seemed to be a gun fanatic. And of course the real fight between Piero and Beppe was over guns.

Taking care of our guns was an obvious concern. But Beppe turned it into a nightly ritual.

In the evenings, when we were all sitting around the television, he would tell stories about his experiences with guns.

One of those evenings, Piero turned and looked at him, and said sharply and harshly: "You have busted our balls long enough, with your guns and your bullshit. Once and for all, can you take this business seriously, or are you going to spend the rest of your life lost in this mental masturbation?"

Before I even realized he was moving, Beppe was across the room, snarling like a wolf, his pistol jammed into Piero's face.

"You piece of shit, you son of a bitch! Now you take it back and stop acting like the little professor, or I'll break your jaw with this! And you just thank your lucky stars that I can't make any noise."

There was a ferocious hatred clearly marked on Beppe's face. A hatred that was oblivious to everything: the moment, the situation, the apartment. Piero was motionless. "Okay, I take it back. Let's not forget why we're here."

There was scorn on his face, but also fear. I could sense it. And Beppe made me uncomfortable too. Beppe stood staring at him.

"You know perfectly well that sooner or later we're going to have it out, the two of us. You have some explaining to do. You know what I'm talking about. And you know that little gentlemen like you should keep their noses clean, instead of causing trouble. I am not planning to see you ruin any more comrades. I don't need your lectures. Do you understand? Hmmm? Is that clear?"

After that evening, Beppe and Piero stopped talking to each other, except when absolutely necessary. And I started to see Beppe differently. His hatred had appeared fierce and authentic, and in that instant his air of complaining and boasting vanished entirely. His hatred was real, deeply felt and even more deeply rooted. He had moved like an animal, and he had attacked like an animal. I was fascinated by the internal energy that had exploded like a bomb. Now, I was sure that I would never be capable of that. In this, I felt that he was truly southern, tougher, more committed, in some sense more ancient than me. Or perhaps I should say, than us. Piero, in comparison with Beppe, had seemed wispy, empty, with his calm careful words.

I sensed this difference between the two of them. And between Beppe and me. Deep down, there was something authentic about him, something spontaneous and vital; something Piero and I did not have.

Piero, in the meanwhile, was no longer sleeping in the same room with me.

He was sleeping in Giovanna's room now, though I never heard them making love. And now I felt completely alone, separated from Piero and everything he did and said. Further and further away. Giovanna hovered around him, discreetly but relentlessly. A partition separated us. Sometimes, now, Giovanna would make dinner for him, but as if it were dinner for all of us.

Our attack went perfectly.

The only thing that went wrong was that Piero fired too soon, but Beppe promptly stepped in and fixed things. I did my part.

Immediately afterward, we went our separate ways, as agreed.

I later learned what Beppe was talking about when he attacked Piero. Piero was suspected of having harmed some comrades through his careless behavior in certain circumstances. I actually think that it was an entirely different issue. Beppe and Piero would have hated each other in any case. They represented two opposite ways of approaching these decisions, this life. And now I felt that I was different from each of them.

The worst thing about this life is the loneliness. And the lack of a woman. And so the most natural thing in the world is to start frequenting prostitutes. At first I felt scorn at my own behavior; later, shame. But now I think that whoring is one of the few things that can make you feel like an ordinary person, one person like any other, a proletarian among proletarians. And it even helps you to make sense of the decisions you have made. Because what is the meaning of your own decisions if it's not the renewed sensation of the rage that has made you different once and for all?

In the daily routine of living underground, it is possible to lose track of that rage, in part because you start to feel self-pity for the living conditions, as if you were a white-collar worker of the revolution. But the time when you really feel like a poor unfortunate soul and nothing more is when you are paying a prostitute.

Of course, you don't start out telling yourself you are going to find a whore. You start wandering around, heading no place in particular. Taking evening strolls is one of my outlets, as being alone makes you thoughtful and keenly aware of your surroundings. Everything that is missing in your relations with others finds a new place in your relationship with things—with cleaning the house, with objects upon which you learn new manual skills you had never thought of before like electric wires, door locks—and your relationship with the climate, the weather, the temperatures, the landscapes, and the stones of the city you live in.

This relationship with the city is a natural thing for someone living underground; you might say that it is a working tool. It was my good luck to preserve in this relationship a part free of obligation, happy, sincerely interested, always, in all of the things that happened around me. And so, despite the fact that shadowing someone turns into a series of long, very long, hikes, often I go out again in the evening, but this time as an idle stroller, and I start wandering again. I like the big boulevards on the outskirts of town, with their lines of plane trees. And these are the same places that are particularly frequented by prostitutes and by the cars of lonely men in search of company. I believe that neither the prostitutes nor the lonely men in their cars pay any attention to the plane trees, and in the final analysis, neither do I, at least not much, even though there are times when I happen to think the opposite. Or maybe I just like to think the opposite.

Under the plane trees, between one tree and the next, open fires and naked legs, and giggling. They are the only girls it is possible for me to meet. They are nothing and no one and therefore that was the only place suitable for me, I thought to myself. And it was also a way of telling myself (with that morbid complacency that is so typical of me), "How low I have fallen." Not because of the prostitutes, of course, but because of my wandering around in a situation that seemed to me to be airless, cramped, confined.

But I would go back, over and over.

There is a swirling, almost frenzied concentration of life around the place. I would never stay for long, because I was always worried there might be a police sweep. And so I would walk through and look around as I went.

One evening I went to the movies. Then (the weather was mild and warm) I cut to the left and walked along the last stretch between my house and the boulevard. I walked a little more slowly than usual, and I was in a good mood. In other words, none of it struck me as particularly grim. And I could hear cheerful laughter, some of it coming from very young people. There was music. Two girls with very short miniskirts had brought a tape player and they were dancing in the street, swiveling their hips. It wasn't much as far as belly-dancing goes. But it was cheerful. And truly cheerful, not that fake cheerfulness that you can recognize a mile away. Both of the girls were from the south.

A crowd of men—well, hardly a crowd, but quite a few considering the hour and the location—was following them. And a swarm of cars, with their doors partly open and their windows rolled down, and in some of them as many as four or five men, pounding their hands on the car doors or rocking back and forth on the seats, urging the girls on, yelling and laughing. I really liked those girls. If it weren't for all the men, I would have approached them.

But I realized that I had a spasmodic desire to make love. A desire so strong that my stomach ached. The next evening, without walking around too much, I went back to them. There was no longer a crowd, and there were two other whores; or maybe it was the same two, but dressed differently and this time without the effect of the music.

I didn't care. I just wanted to fuck. I practically chose at random. No haggling. We went behind the tree and I took her standing up, with all my clothes on, and I came right away. I never even looked at her, but I could feel her under my hands, like I had never felt anyone before in my life. Sometimes I masturbate at home. And I read a lot of pornographic magazines. Some of the photographs I cut out and paste to the wall; and from time to time I replace them with others. And so I feel like something of a truck driver and something of a playboy. Once I fell in love with one of my comrades, but she didn't fall in love with me. It happened about a year or so ago. My encounter with Elena was decisive, and it interrupted for the first time this solitary and neurotic experience of living undergound.

With Anna I had always played the traditional man's role. With Elena (finally?) the opposite was the case.

Last spring, we had a very complicated action on our hands. To make things worse, it was boring. Moreover, none of us was truly committed to it. In the end, something happened that should never happen: we tried to execute the action, and at the last minute the car that was supposed to wait for us got lost en route and forced us to abort everything. In that situation, we had all basically come unglued. We asked for a meeting. Two people were sent out to meet with us, and one of them was Elena, a great big girl with a strong southern accent, of proletarian origin, tough and determined. Or at least that is how she appears and what she is trying to convey. Elena is her nom de guerre; I still don't know her real name. She would smoke, work, smoke some more. One or two packs a day. She slept at my apartment, the only place that was available. She would take down the pictures of nude women, while I—in part as a game, in part as a form of provocation—would regularly put up others. But her feminine presence began to become evident in the apartment.

I don't think that I was ever attracted to Elena physically.

My type is still Anna, really. What I liked about Anna was the fine air she had of being an educated and well-mannered person, her serious but elegant clothing. Elena, on the other hand, does nothing to adorn her body. It is a way to reiterate, I think, that she is—has to be—what she does.

During an action, something changes in her. She becomes chilly and determined; her expression becomes very intense. I have never seen her hands shake. She never talks about her life, her past, her feelings. She cultivates an image of unattainability.

And so we lived together. Slowly, subtly, I could feel her establish her presence in the apartment: a daily presence, which I couldn't identify but which I was willing to accept. Slowly, subtly, I grew to count on this situation. I would seek out opportunities to talk to her, moving with her as she went from room to room. I would start a conversation, talking about nothing in particular, and she would answer in similar terms. She would concede her time to me, but it was clearly a concession. I wanted a relationship, not a gift. And so I started talking about politics, and this drew her in to a greater degree. But I found myself swept up into long, all-absorbing debates from which I could not disentangle myself.

Elena is absolutely intolerable in this aspect. She knows everything; she has studied everything and has met everybody. But even that was okay by me. After so much solitude, her powerful presence made it possible for me to stop thinking about myself. That is how it started. Slowly, subtly.

The apartment that I had rented was, in fact, still is,

very small. There is my bedroom, and the other room, which is everything—living room, kitchen, parlor, den. I had not furnished it before, nor did Elena after she got there. I had bought furniture from the UPIM[18] department store, an Indian print bed cover, a few posters, a round table made of clear plastic that I bought at a sale. Just enough to make it into a normal, presentable apartment, in case anyone happened to come in. But I never did any more than that, nor did I want to.

And neither did Elena. But her presence made the apartment seem less empty, if only because it was more lived-in. I started buying groceries for both of us. In the morning I would leave early. She would stay in the apartment and do her paperwork—inventories, clipping newspapers, filing, reading. In fact, we started to live as a couple. I felt as if with her I was in one of those relationships without passion or enthusiasm, which, depending on how you look at it, seems either dead inside or, in another sense, capable of offering peace and serenity. For a few months Elena and I constituted a full-fledged autonomous operative base. For that matter, she had been sent to this city precisely to consolidate and reinforce our group, and she worked single-mindedly toward this goal.

The end of this unusual relationship and the realization that I was in love came at the same time. There was a plenary meeting, in another city. We took the train together with a familiarity that already smacked of cohabitation. At the end of the meeting Elena calmly went off to sleep somewhere else. It is obvious that you can't ask where or how or why in this kind of a situation.

But it was pretty easy for me to understand, without too much discussion, that in reality Elena had no politicial reasons, strictly personal considerations.

Elena has absolutely no interest in having a husband.

Every so often I still see her. We say hello in perfect fondness.

It's true. She's right. I can't deny her a stroll in the village. Mamma woke me this morning with a hand stroking my hair.

"Hello sweetheart. Here's your coffee." In her voice you could hear that sort of commotion that she always has when she pretends, inside, that I am still a child. The worst thing about my mother is how obvious she is. I know, minute by minute, exactly what she is thinking. But not because I know her particularly well; rather, because everything she thinks is obvious. So if she comes to wake me up and strokes my hair, you can be certain that in her head she is thinking, "There's my little boy." If, on the street, she says, "Look what a beautiful baby," she is thinking, "One day maybe I'll have a grandchild," and if she brings me a cup of coffee, she is thinking, "How does he get through the day when I'm not there?"

And for that matter, maybe that's a nice thing about her. Cars are mass-produced, after all, and people generally like cars.

"What are you planning to do this morning?"

"I don't know, Mamma. My eyes aren't even open yet."

"You're right darling. Drink your coffee and wash your face. I'll get you some breakfast in the other room."

"Mamma, for the millionth time, I don't eat breakfast. I only drink coffee."

"But you're here on vacation, and . . ."

"Mamma, we have this discussion every year."

"You're right, dear. I'm sorry. I'll see you after you're up."

She is just so irritating. And yet there is something about this way she has of treating me that is painful. What could it be?

Now she wants me to go shop for groceries with her in the village, so she can show me off to her girlfriends. She will take me to see all the shopkeepers: "Signor Mario, do you remember my son?" "Of course, Signora. I haven't seen you in a while," says Mario, gripping my hand. "What are you doing, what are you up to?" he goes on. Mamma answers for me: "He's in Rome now, you know?" "In Rome? Good Lord, Signora, these young people. Just think, I've never been to Rome."

And after all, why not? I am here on vacation. I have to be here, for them, and to blunt their suspicions. I should just act like any son staying with his parents on holiday. What do I care? I certainly have no need to reject this sort of thing now, as if I were some young rebel. The decisions I have already made are much more far-reaching and radical.

And so we set off for the village.

Mamma has on a flowery sleeveless dress. Her arms are tanned, there is a little cellulite on her upper arms.

"Mamma, how long have we been coming here?"

As soon as I ask the question I wish I hadn't. My mother almost jumps; she is so accustomed to my silent, quarrelsome presence. And now I have actually asked a question that reveals I have memories.

"Why, dearest, since you were eight years old. Don't you remember? We came here for the first time in your grandfather's Fiat 600; your grandmother was still alive . . ."

Her eyes glisten at this opportunity to pour over my head all the fake honey that she carries around with her. Her eyes take on that stereotypical expression; she calls me dearest every chance she gets. I just can't stand it. But I need to resign myself, forget about it. I just need to be careful not to offer her another opening, another straw to grab at.

God damn her cellulite, like she is some old biddy.

"That was when your father was having money problems, because they had shut down the company. That was before the civil service examination. At any rate, we were living on money from your grandfather . . . "

She chatters on relentlessly all the way down to the village.

I'm thinking about other things. But I feel good. I have always liked this mountain air. Maybe not right here: there are too many geraniums growing on the balconies and windowboxes; too many satiny lawns, as if they were plastic. But it's a nice quiet place. And I have spent some happy times here. This is where I learned to ice skate, this is where I hunted for strawberries in the woods. Here I could keep a dog—an impossibility in the city, in my mother's apartment. With her inevitable list of things that you can and cannot do. Always the schoolteacher.

And the schoolteacher goes on. "Ever since your aunt took that terrible fall, she has never really recovered.

Actually, ever since your grandfather died ma̶
years ago she has never quite known what to ᵥ
herself. She tried to devote herself to taking care c̶
father. But you know how independent-minded ᵥ
father can be . . ." Independent-minded is another waᵧ
saying that she would never allow her supremacy in tḥ
home to be undermined by anyone else.

"And over the years, your father has just become more
and more independent. He has always had a difficult personality, but now you should see him. With the fact that
he is ready to retire, he is always finding excuses to stay
out. He goes to the Veteran's Club all the time. Sometimes we go together, sometimes he goes alone. He says
that he needs to make all the friends he has never had all
his life . . ."

It's true. My father is about to retire. What will he do
now, and who are these friends? In my whole life I have
never seen him once with anybody but my mother. My
father's friends. How ridiculous. Maybe he is seeing
another woman. Or else he is playing bocce.

Suddenly, a memory of my father surfaces in my
mind. A veterans' club, with a pergola and little tables in
the shade; next to it, in the bright sunlight, two bocce
courts. Sometimes my father would take me there.
Maybe it was when my mother was at the hairdresser's.
He would leave me with a sheet of paper and an
orangeade on the little table, and he would play in the
neighboring bocce courts. The bocce players would yell
as they tossed the balls.

My father. Him too. He never talks. But doesn't that
make him just like me?

"So there are times when I just don't know what to say to him. Because with age, you know, people get to be very good at hiding their feelings. He was hoping for that promotion, and I think that even now he is hoping for it. But if he ever does get that promotion, it will just be a way of sending him into retirement. And I think that he feels basically still very young and full of energy."

Young, full of energy. I never thought of using these words to describe those two. And yet there must have been a time when they made love. The two of them, always covered in dressing gowns, pajamas; doors shut with the key turned. And yet they must have done it.

I suddenly feel as if I am going to faint. "Mamma, let's stop for just a second, please." Now she is worried, I can tell. But I really don't feel very good. "What's the matter? Let's go the café. Don't worry. Should I go get the car, so you don't have to walk back up?" "No, Mamma, don't worry. It's the altitude, that's all. You know that, don't you?"

In the main square are the beautiful trees that I remember so well. It is nice to sit in their shade. Mamma has set me down here, she has ordered a strawberry granita for me. "Now I'll go finish my shopping by myself, and I'll come get you afterward," she said. But she wasn't obnoxious. She didn't try to cover me with honey.

She was genuinely concerned.

My father, my mother, my aunt, me. What does all this have to do with me, now, here, right here and now?

I have been here for three days, and as always it seems

that I have been here for so much longer. It is certainly an effect of the mountains. The hours get much longer, the days stretch away into the possibility of having all the time you want.

In the morning I wake up early, unlike in the city, because I go to sleep early. What can you do up here after you drink a few beers?

I sleep well. I sleep like I haven't slept in a long time. I feel relaxed and safe in this apartment. Unfortunately, that is how it is. And I say *unfortunately* because this makes me realize the degree to which what I consider routine is actually extremely tense. I even feel relaxed because of all the stupid crap that my mother insists on keeping in my room.

I wake up with the light pouring in from the roof window, I turn over on the mattress (a woolen mattress, what luxury), and I open one eye. I see the fringework dangling from a flag I had as a kid. The smell in this room is familiar to me too. Maybe it's the smell of my own body.

Yesterday morning I played cards with my aunt, on a little table in the garden. The sun was baking the back of my neck. It left me feeling weak. But what a pleasure not to have any strength and not to need any.

My aunt is quite a character. I have always liked her. Yesterday she said something incredibly mean about this woman who is our neighbor, and she basically said it within earshot, and when she saw that I was embarrassed, she said, "Calm down, sweetie, she grows a new layer of thick skin every year."

There is no point in trying to hide it from myself. I like it here. And I am curious about my parents. I am sort of ashamed, not for being curious now, but for how super-ficial I have been in the past.

As parents, they still irritate me immensely. But they are also people, just people. And they aren't stupid people. They have their problems, they have a few things of their own. And when I say that I have changed, I am referring to these thoughts that come to me, thoughts that I never used to have. Now I am happy to remember, I am happy to have a place to come to, I like the sun on the back of my neck, and today I'll even go play soccer.

As for my parents, I have one more question.

They don't have much. I have more than they do. Of this I am certain. Or maybe I'm wrong. And what if the life I have chosen is every bit as pathetic, what if there are aspects that are equally paltry, and I just can't see it?

I think I'll go play soccer.

My mother continues not to pry into my affairs, except for stupid details.

What's going on?

Yesterday I went with her to buy groceries for the third time. This was the last time. Tomorrow I am leaving again. These outings, after the first day, have become a tacit opportunity for us to talk, though we don't actually say much to each other.

So now there is something like an understanding between us. I don't want to talk about complicity, but there is something like that going on here.

What on earth does she imagine? Certainly, I have an almost pathologically suspicious mind, but I don't think

I am wrong in this case. She is more relaxed about acting happy to have me here; she doesn't drive me crazy anymore. The way she treats me seems to have equal components of concern and protectiveness, with the tone of someone discussing a very important matter. If I had a fever, she would be frantic. At least that is how it used to be. And instead, now she talks about general subjects, acts as cheerful as can be, but carefully avoids asking me anything about the life I lead. Yesterday morning, while she was telling me to pick out the apples I like best and rattling on about another aunt of mine, who is never satisfied, even with her famous son, my cousin—he is always trotted out whenever a comparison is needed to show me at a disadvantage, the son who is always doing everything right in life—she made the following comment: "And after all, you know, I think that at a certain point children grow and you just have to accept that fact. I don't know if I have been lucky or unlucky with you, and I don't even know if I did everything I could for you. But now I have stopped worrying about it. Whatever you do now is your business. All that we can do is to make sure that there is always a place where you can be happy, when you want it."

Then she changed the subject, blithely continuing to say mean things about the other aunt, the one "who is never satisfied with anything." I interpreted all this in the only way possible. And maybe I am wrong. Maybe they are all just fantasies.

As lovely as it is to climb up to the mountains by bus, it is just as horrible to head down. The bus takes the curves slowly on the way up; it doesn't lurch sickeningly, and you always have the mountains in front of you. On the way down, the bus swerves and tilts in a frightening manner, and you feel like you are going to crash, or in any case arrive as white as a sheet, and the air becomes increasingly dense and polluted. I am going to sleep all the way back to Milan. Tomorrow, it's back to work.

The letters that Anna and I write each other had become like the last periods of time we spent together—vague and infrequent.

She would write me in a firm round hand: "I'm fine, I'm studying."

Then she would take up her stories. Giorgio this, Lucia that. The other evening I saw everybody from high school at the concert. They all asked me about you and they told me to say "get in touch." Then, only at the end of each letter, is a distinctive phrase, typical of Anna: "I think about you more than you can imagine."

The phrase struck me as uniquely hers, and it seemed to contain many messages.

I would write her equally vague letters. Once I sent her a book; every so often I would call her on the phone.

Only one letter was so fundamental that I almost memorized it.

"In reality—even though it has been a mutual decision, tacitly agreed upon—it's been a long, long time since we last spoke. At first, I had great misgivings about this new way of being together. We have drifted apart, it's true. I felt like you were distant; you seemed intentionally evasive. You shouldn't think that I failed to notice your efforts to maintain distance. And after all, we had been through a bad experience, that weekend in Genoa that I had hoped could free us from the constant anger; it all went wrong, and it hurt me badly. We had spent a happy part of our lives in that house. And you know how much I love that house. So I figured that you needed some freedom, some more time for yourself. I guess we have just always been together too much. We have known each other since school; we've known each other forever, it seems. I suspected that you had another woman, or other women. And I had to decide what to do quickly. And so I came to realize that you mattered a great deal to me; I found that I could accept your desire for freedom. And I discovered how much I loved you. Even if now I am writing you a truly ridiculous letter. Am I right? Am I understanding your life as it is? Or even now is there something I am failing to understand?

"I am only writing you these things now for a very simple reason. Despite everything, this period has been important for me, too. Maybe I needed for you to force the first move, as you always do. In this, as always, I am relying on you. And yet, after being forced to face your desire for freedom, I find myself being forced to deal with my own desire for freedom as well.

"Do you realize, in reality, just how much time we spent together, the degree to which our involvement in politics kept us in a cage, in a life that focused entirely on ourselves and our friends, and our certainties?

"Among the many things for which I blame you, there is one in particular. You were never willing to value the work I had chosen for myself. When I chose a field of study for which I was going to have to work hard, you made fun of me. Then you stopped, but you always had hundreds of subtle methods to keep me from pursuing this thing that mattered so much to me. Most important, you were scornful.

"When our relationship subsided, I slowly began to rediscover time for myself. I was hurting over you, it's true, but my days slowly started to fill up with other things.

"I am beginning to feel that I am something, someone, a concrete existence.

"I go to the hospital; I only give injections now but I work with real people, little old ladies for the most part and useless work in a sense, but I like them, I feel like I can do something to help them. Then I have friends. Doctors, like me. Some of them have absolutely no political experience, they are just 'democratic' fools, as you would say. But we go to see movies together; we talk about real things, things that matter. I haven't been able to tolerate certain other types of discussion for a while now. Sometimes, I feel so happy that I feel guilty toward you. In some sense, for me to exist, you had to disappear.

"And so I write you. Now I feel as if we are moving into a difficult situation. Up till now, the ties that have held us together have been sufficient. But now I am changing. And you aren't here. Where and how will we ever see each other again? Will we ever see each other again? Can we stop behaving like children? Can we quit indulging in this love of freedom, so brutal and self-centered, and find each other again, respectfully?

"You haven't given me any serious signs that you exist

for some time now. What are you really doing? Who have you become in the meanwhile?

"It's time to see each other. It's time. We may not recognize each other anymore."

Of course, I wrote back with a postcard. It was a perfect point to break off entirely. "Who says that we won't see each other again? You're funny, with all this serious talk."

By return mail, I received another, very short letter.

"There is not much I can add."

I called her on the phone. Festive exclamations: "Hello! How are you?" And a sweeping emotion that I could hardly conceal.

"Are you coming up? Do you want to come with me to the house by the sea? Now, you know, my folks are much more relaxed about letting me use it. My dad says hello; so does my mother. How are things in Rome? Do you have enough money?"

"Sure, we'll get together soon. I still don't know when. I'll write you, okay? I have to go; I'm out of coins."

"All right," she agreed, tersely.

I hung up the receiver. I put in another token for the periodic phone call to reassure my mother. And then I went back to my apartment.

I had reached a point where I was working at full capacity. I couldn't turn back; I didn't want to turn back. I never wrote her again. She never wrote me again.

Milan is a city unlike any other
Where you can be great and unassuming, someone
    and no one at all,

189

Where time teaches you forms of patience that are
    inaccessible elsewhere.
Milan is a city of protest marches and funerals,
Funerals that seem like protest marches and protest
    marches that seem like carnivals,
And carnivals that seem like rioting in the streets.
Milan in the evening, when you walk out into the
    streets, down into the Metropolitana stations, and
    up into the apartments,
And it's cold in a way that makes you feel warm,
And the houses seem like churches.
Milan is a city of dawning mornings
With grim-faced factory workers riding bicycles
And young factory workers who ride in the
    Metropolitana
And bundles of pink sports dailies on the ground by
    the newsstands, still closed for the night.
Milan is a city to walk through
To capture the smells, the noises, the pain,
To shadow the steps and the fatigue.
To shadow enemies and accomplices.

And I'm here to shadow my father
Who's dressed in gray, white in the face,
An opera singer and a veteran of the War,
And he is there shadowing his office manager
Who has two or three villas and a certain love for
    windsurfing,
And the office manager is shadowing the doorman
Who has lots of lovers and a big cock,
And then there's someone shadowing me,

I've never seen him but I know he's there,
I've never seen his face, but I can guess what face
  it is.

I can sense him behind me in the Galleria and in a
  movie theater in the industrial hinterland
Among the students in a night school
And at the city library and in a crazy discotheque.
Whether he is my father or my betrayer,
My carabiniere or my guardian angel,
My weariness and my exhaustion,
My hatred and my bitterness.
Whether it is my comrades of today or those of the past,
My teachers or my priests
Or my endless, infinite thoughts.
Whether they are my tired ideas or my hallucinations,
My dreams or my passions,
Or maybe these tight shoes or this collar that doesn't
  fasten.
Or this desire for everything and this fear of nothing,
This listless desire or this soporose hatred.
Whether it is or it isn't,
There's always someone behind me in the pizzeria
Who eats with feigned cheerfulness and while
  feigning sadness
Can guess at my madness.

ENDNOTES

1. Adriano Celentano is an Italian singer and song-writer, universally loved but especially on the left. This song—*Azzurro*—is about loss and loneliness and summertime, and dates from the 1960s.

2. Corto Maltese is a cult adventure comic strip by the late Hugo Pratt. A Clint Eastwood-like adventurer, Corto Maltese's father was a British sailor born in Cornwall; his mother was a Spanish gypsy from Seville. His official residence was Antigua, in the Antilles; but his only known home was in Hong Kong. The fictional character Corto Maltese was born in 1887, on Malta, and disappeared in 1936, fighting in the Spanish Civil War. During his adventuresome life he traveled to Argentina, Shanghai, Yemen, and Russia; among the friends he traveled with were Butch Cassidy, the Sundance Kid, Jack London, and Rasputin (yes, Rasputin). Hugo Pratt was born in Italy in 1927 and died in France in 1995. Umberto Eco compared him to Dumas.

3. The Autonomia is a broad term covering a confederation of diverse extraparliamentary left-wing groups; extraparliamentary means that they scorned the elected government and worked through "other" means: ranging from mass demonstrations to terrorism.

4. Youth Groups were loosely organized associations, found on both the left and the right.

5. Lotta Continua (Continuous Struggle) was a left-wing

extraparliamentary movement and daily newspaper of enormous importance; it was dissolved by its founder, Adriano Sofri, in the mid-70s, because of the increasingly violent nature of political conflict in Italy.

6. In the Italian, Giorgio says Maria Theresa instead of Marie Antoinette; a particularly touching error. Maria Theresa was in fact the archduchess of Austria, and played an important role in Italian politics and culture; Giorgio means to refer to Marie Antoinette, one of Maria Theresa's children, guillotined in the French Revolution, during the Terror. I have substituted Marie Antoinette for her mother in the English.

7. Giulio Andreotti, seven times prime minister of Italy, in 2002 convicted for ordering the murder of a journalist, though acquitted for actual Mafia membership a few years previous. Perhaps the most powerful politician in the ruling Christian Democratic party, Andreotti was a favorite villain of the left; their pet name for him was "Beelzebub," or "Lord of the Flies," both nicknames for Lucifer.

8. Suspense film 1957, directed by Louis Malle, with Jeanne Moreau; also known as *Lift to the Scaffold* or *Frantic*. Man plotting murder is caught in broken elevator, foiling his alibi for a "perfect crime."

9. Quasi-anarchistic organization that included at least one member of the Situationist International (Riccardo d'Este) and was loosely affiliated with Italian Luddites; disbanded in 1973.

10. M.L.S, Movimento Lavoratori per il Socialismo, literally, Socialist Workers Movement, a neo-Stalinist movement on the extraparliamentary left.

11. Left-wing organization, more mainstream with some electoral activity.

12. The Italian equivalent of the *Wall Street Journal* or the *Financial Times.*

13. See endnote 5.

14. Extraparliamentary left-wing group.

15. A revolutionary (not merely extraparliamentary) left-wing group.

16. Ugo Pecchioli, a leader of the Italian Communist Party, greatly hated by the Autonomi.

17. Frate Mitra, or Brother Machinegun, was the name given by the popular press to Silvano Girotto, one of the earliest turncoat informers on the left and specifically the Red Brigades.

18. Major department store chain, comparable to JC Penney or Sears in the U.S.

CPSIA information can be obtained
at www.ICGtesting.com
Printed in the USA
BVOW03s0058120417
R7903000002B/R79030PG480698BVX2B/1/P